BURNING LIGHTS

BELLA CHAGALL

BURNING LIGHTS

THIRTY-SIX DRAWINGS BY
MARC CHAGALL

SCHOCKEN BOOKS

First SCHOCKEN PAPERBACK edition 1962
Seventh Printing, 1974

Translated by Norbert Guterman

Library of Congress Catalog Card No. 46-8515

Manufactured in the United States of America

CONTENTS

*Bella Chagall was born in Vitebsk, Russia, in a Has-
sidic family, on December 15, 1895. Her parents
were Samuel Noah Rosenfeld and Alta, née Levant.
She was the youngest of seven children.*

*After graduating from the Vitebsk Gymnasium for
girls, she became a student in the Faculty of Letters
at the University of Moscow in 1912. In her student
years she contributed to the Moscow newspaper* Utro
Rossii.

*In 1914 Marc Chagall returned from Paris to his
native Vitebsk. Marc and Bella Chagall, who had been
childhood friends, married in Vitebsk on July 25,
1915.*

*In 1922 the Chagall family settled in Paris. Bella
translated into French and edited Marc Chagall's auto-
biography "My Life."*

*Bella Chagall visited Palestine in 1931 and Vilna in
1935. The contact with Jewish life impressed her so
deeply that she began to write in Yiddish.*

*Bella Chagall died at Cranberry Lake, N. Y., on
September 2, 1944.*

HERITAGE

IT IS an odd thing: a desire comes to me to write, and to write in my faltering mother tongue, which, as it happens, I have not spoken since I left the home of my parents.

Far as my childhood years have receded from me, I now suddenly find them coming back to me, closer and closer to me, so near, they could be breathing into my mouth.

I see myself so clearly—a plump little thing, a tiny girl running all over the place, pushing my way from one door through another, hiding like a curled-up little worm with my feet up on our broad window sills.

My father, my mother, the two grandmothers, my handsome grandfather, my own and outside families, the comfortable and the needy, weddings and funerals, our streets and gardens—all this streams before my eyes like the deep waters of our Dvina.

My old home is not there any more. Everything is gone, even dead.

My father, may his prayers help us, has died. My

mother is living—and God alone knows whether she still lives—in an un-Jewish city that is quite alien to her. The children are scattered in this world and the other, some here, some there. But each of them, in place of his vanished inheritance, has taken with him, like a piece of his father's shroud, the breath of the parental home.

I am unfolding my piece of heritage, and at once there rise to my nose the odors of my old home.

My ears begin to sound with the clamor of the shop and the melodies that the rabbi sang on holidays. From every corner a shadow thrusts out, and no sooner do I touch it than it pulls me into a dancing circle with other shadows. They jostle one another, prod me in the back, grasp me by the hands, the feet, until all of them together fall upon me like a host of humming flies on a hot day. I do not know where to take refuge from them. And so, just once, I want very much to wrest from the darkness a day, an hour, a moment belonging to my vanished home.

But how does one bring back to life such a moment?

Dear God, it is so hard to draw out a fragment of bygone life from fleshless memories! And what if they should flicker out, my lean memories, and die away together with me?

I want to rescue them.

I recall that you, my faithful friend, have often in affection begged me to tell you about my life in the time before you knew me. So I am writing for you.

[10]

Our town is even dearer to you than to me. And you, with your full heart, will understand even what I shall not succeed in telling.

Only one thing torments me. My sweet little daughter, who spent only a single year of her life in my parental home—and this as a one-year-old child—will she understand me? Let us hope that she will.

Saint-Dié, France, 1939

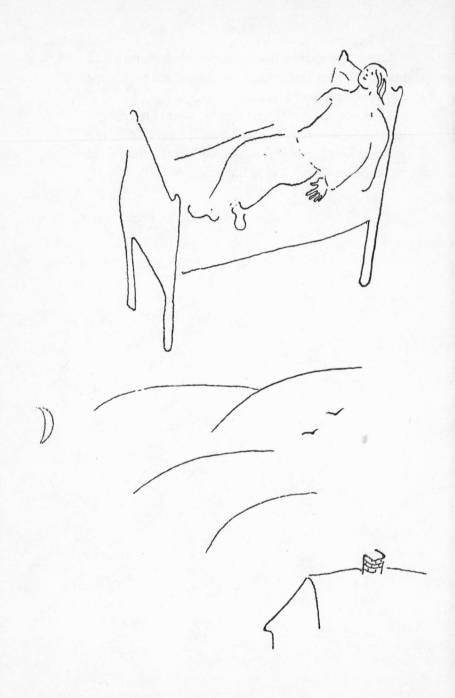

THE COURTYARD

IN THE daytime after dinner our apartment is deserted. Everyone has gone out. A big place, and no one there. One might as well bring in the goat from the courtyard or the chickens in the cage under the stove.

Only from the kitchen there comes the clatter of dishes being washed there.

"Have you swept the dining room?" The voice in the kitchen pushes out Sasha with a long broom in her hand.

"What are you doing here?" she assails me.

"Nothing!" I answer as always.

"Get out, I have to sweep the room."

"Who is stopping you? Go ahead, sweep it!"

She sweeps up the floor, and with the rubbish she sweeps out the last voices that have sounded in the room. The dining room has gone cold now.

The walls suddenly are old, their faded paper strikes the eye. The empty table stands like something superfluous in the middle of the room. It seems to me that I too am a superfluous thing here.

Where shall I take myself? I wander about in the house. I come to the bedroom. The little beds, all covered and smooth, stand there uninviting. Who would lie down on them in the middle of the day?

Father's and mother's high beds are forbidding with their nickel gleam. The nickel bars in front, in back, their thick ball tops, guard them like sentries on watch.

When one comes closer to them, the nickel shoots at one with its metallic glint. When I look into it, my face is distorted, my nose is split. I run away from it and I bump against a locked door. I have quite forgotten that there is a parlor.

The door is always locked. I am always afraid of that room. Since my brother's wedding, when for the sake of the bride's family, the old Viennese chairs were replaced with new, soft furniture, the parlor has become unfamiliar—it seems to have separated itself from our apartment.

In the parlor it is dark. On the sofa lies a dense moss of thick green plush. When anyone sits down on it, even if it is only the cat, its steel springs utter a groan, as though they were always sick and could not bear to have anybody press them.

The rug too is green, as if grass were growing on it. And the few pink flowers embroidered on it ward one off; I fancy that the shadow of someone's feet may be lying on the rug and will not let anyone step on it.

Even the tall, long mirror has turned green. Night and day the green furniture is reflected in it.

An old palm stands wretched near the window, drying up in the green gloom. The window is always closed, curtained; the palm never sees the sun.

Instead of the sun, there shine for it a couple of bronze candelabras on their high stands in the corners. Into the candelabras are stuck short white candles that are never lighted. From the ceiling hangs a chandelier, also of bronze; only the dangling white crystals make it alive. At night the palm thinks that something shines for it from the ceiling sky, and that little stars glimmer down from the crystal pendants.

It must be stronger than iron to hold out day after day, months, years.

No one stops in the parlor. Everyone just quickly crosses it like a bridge leading from one room to another.

True, father prays there in the morning in his talis and tefillin. Perhaps he thinks that he goes out to pray on a green meadow. And during the day when he goes there to look for a book in the bookcase, he does not even glance at this piece of furniture.

The bookcase is the only old piece of furniture that has remained in the parlor. It has been left where it always stood, in a corner next to the door. Because it is crammed full of books, it probably could not be moved. Absorbed in its books, it stands there as though it had no relation to all of the life of the house.

I approach it as though it were an old relative; I touch it with a light tap, and its short legs begin to creak. It is hard for them to support the whole book-case.

I peer through its doors. There is shelf upon shelf, each like a separate oratory. Here, in black boards, hard on one another, turning their backs to the glass, stand tall, lean gemaras, like old Jews lined up along a wall for the Shemoneh Esreh.

On another shelf thick bibles and machzors, sid-durs, and psalters spread themselves. So many women's prayer books are piled on the lowest shelves that one almost hears a murmur coming from there.

I fancy that all the books are upset because I am gazing at them. I run away; they cry after me as my old grandfather shouted at mother, asking why they were teaching me Russian, why they did not rather hire a teacher to teach me Yiddish.

"Oh," I suddenly remind myself, "my little teacher will be coming soon, with whom I fall asleep over the alphabet." I must save myself from him.

"Where are you running like mad, Bashke?" Sasha asks, stopping me.

"What business is that of yours?" I fling back at her. "Not anywhere."

I run out into the courtyard.

The balcony, although of iron, bends under my feet. The bars are narrow and widely spaced, my heels get stuck in the openings. The wall is high.

From below, from above, stairs run up and down, one twisting above the other. The handrails hold them up like chains.

The uppermost stairs lead up to the glass-roofed attic; a photographer lives there. The lowest stairs wind down and stop almost in the middle of the courtyard.

There, under the very lowest step, is my nook. There I play, there is my shop, there I dry my cakes of wet sand. There lie my tin cans that once held sardines; now they are filled with groats, oatmeal, all kinds of little stones, shards, pieces of colored glass—everything that I find in the courtyard and everything that I save from being trampled upon by strangers' feet.

The courtyard, small and square, is like a box closed in by high walls. There a world of people is living. The sun does not come there. Above, a patch of sky gleams. Shadows of light fall from the walls.

All around are the windows and doors of the big Hotel Brozi. Each window belongs to a separate apartment. From each a different head sticks out, and every day it is a different one. As soon as a new guest arrives, the curtain is lowered in the window.

"You see, little miss, new guests have arrived," says the baker, who has come into the courtyard to cool off. He points to the curtained window. "Very likely they are just up from the train, and they are taking a rest. You won't be noisy in the courtyard, little girl, eh?" he says to me. He swallows a breath of fresh air, and goes quietly back to the kitchen.

Noisy, I?

I do not have time to ask him. He might at least tell me why all the travelers are tired. After all, it is the train that runs, not they.

The old baker knows that I am afraid of him, afraid of his flour-smeared face, of his high white cap and white smock.

I, noisy? Don't I sit quietly on the steps? It is noisy enough in the courtyard without me. The hotel servants scurry around there like mice. Back and forth—one goes out, another goes in, one drags something, another fills or empties something. Jewish women come in from the street to sell eggs, chickens, cream. This makes a hubbub.

The hens cluck. The cat crawls underfoot, seeking a morsel of food. The dog comes running, his tongue hanging out, his tail up in the air. That frightens the cock and he tries to squirm out of the hands that hold him. The cat hides in a corner.

The dog runs about over the whole courtyard, sniffs everywhere, as though he were the chief steward, who must give an accounting of everything to the proprietor. The attendants jostle one another, exchange taunts.

"Buy the cock," the street peddler begs them.

"Go with your cock to all the black years! He is older than Terah!"

"God be with you! May my hands and feet dry up if I am cheating you!"

"Get out of here, you old witch! Do you hear what you're told? If you don't—"

The old woman, as well as the cock in her hand, falls silent. She stands there waiting: perhaps the goy's wrath will subside. Now he is taking someone else to task.

"Where are you crowding in, you devil? You've rolled my barrel right into the mud!"

"Who, what? You must be drunk, you dog's snout! You're picking a fight with everybody. Just wait, I'll show you—"

"Hey, Piotr, Stepan!" Someone calls to them from the kitchen. "May you both burn! Have you peeled the potatoes? The cook is waiting—"

The two goyim separate and run back.

"Piotr, take the cock with you!" The peddler runs after them. "Show it in the kitchen. Just have it roasted—you'll see, you'll lick your fingers!"

No one listens to her. She screams her heart out. Head hanging, she shoves her cock back into her basket.

"Gla-a-sha-a-a-a! Where are you, eh?" Suddenly there comes a call from the window, long drawn out, like a whistle. "Gla-a-sha-a-a-a! Come here! Where have you got lost? The lady in Number One is calling for you!"

Only the hotel laundresses, who iron linen at the

open windows, do not revile one another. They sing, as though the heat of their irons were warming their hearts. Sometimes it seems that they are sobbing. Their sad melody goes on and on, just as the pile of linen thrown to them for ironing never grows less.

Suddenly the two young daughters of the landlord run into the courtyard. They squeal with laughter. I jump toward them, and jump away again at once. The girls are spitting something—for a moment I think it is blood. They are cracking freshly cooked red lobsters with their teeth.

"What are you doing? Fie!" I think in fancy that they are swallowing bloody mice.

"Ivan!" they shout into the open stable. "Lead out the horses, we are going for a ride at once!"

In the stable, two tall horses begin to neigh, answering their call.

The horses' black, fat rumps glisten as though they had been polished with wax. Little tears of sweat roll down their hide. Steaming, they kick up their legs, shake their manes. Blindly they grope for the bag of oats that the coachman has hung on the wall. They poke their heads into the bag and fall asleep there. Only their long necks throb and bend, like trumpets thrust into the air.

The coachman's hair and boots also glisten with grease. He stands by the horses, strokes them.

"Ivan," I say to him, "haven't you just come back from town?"

"*Sluzhba nie druzhba*—a servant is not a friend. Isn't it so, my horse?" says Ivan, giving the horse a vigorous slap on the flank.

The horses each stick out an eye from the bag to throw a glance at the coachman. Why doesn't he let them eat? They vent their anger on the flies, lashing out with their tails.

Their overheated legs cannot stay still. Their knees bend under them, then straighten out. Their hoofs scrape the ground; they are trying to find out what lies underfoot. Only a little while ago they were galloping across the town. In a flash they dashed through one street after another. And here in the stable, as soon as they stir, there is the drag of the heavy iron chains by which they are tethered to the beam.

"H-r-r-r," they whinny while they eat.

"M-m-mu—m-m-mu," answers the cow from her shed, and keeps on mooing.

I cannot restrain myself and I run to her.

The horses' stable is at least open, they always have fresh air. But the cow is locked up like a thief in prison.

A beautiful red animal—and people are ashamed of her. Her shed is dark, dirty; it is situated in the corner of the yard, next to the garbage box. Its walls are thin. The slightest wind blows through them. Rain spatters in through the cracks. A large hole in the door serves the cow as a little window. Through it I gaze at her. She lies there without strength, her belly and legs sunk into the dirty straw. A swarm of flies are biting her. The cow does not stir; she might be a pile of garbage.

Is she really such a lazybones? She does hear the humming of the flies, and occasionally, reluctantly, she raises her thin, long tail, all caked with mud, and drives away the flies. Of her entire body, only the head is alive.

Now one ear lifts, now the other droops. The cow perceives every noise that comes from the courtyard. In her quiet, day-long sadness, she slowly ruminates each sound separately. She has a wet, weeping snout. Her eyes are full of tears that stay in the corners. Only now and then a tear rolls down her long nose. I cannot endure her gaze. Like a heavy stone, it weighs on my heart, as though it were my fault that she is locked up.

"M-m-mu—m-m-mu," I whisper to her through the dark hole.

"M-m-mu—m-m-mu," she answers heavily and slowly, and now stares at me with quiet joy because someone remembers her. But she knows that it is not I who will release her, who will open the door of her shed.

So again her head droops sadly, and she lies there until the hour of milking comes. As soon as she sniffs the odor of the mush that they prepare for her with boiling water, she gathers up her pendulous belly, her legs, her udder, and takes up her post at the door. She stands there snuffing the air, and waits, listening to every step.

She hears Sasha throwing into the trough big pieces of beets with long leaves, boiled potatoes, carrots. She hears the maid pouring boiling water into it, mixing the fodder, so that she, the cow, should not be scalded. Her tongue begins to hang out. She thumps on the door with her horns.

As soon as Sasha opens the shed, the cow runs out, nimble, alive, stamping her feet, rolling her sides. Crusts of dried mud drop from her. She does not look at anyone. Only when she passes the carriage standing without its horses in the middle of the courtyard, the cow offhandedly gives it a push. It is her way of jostling the horses because they get much more attention than she does.

She crawls into the trough up to her neck, laps the water, chews the greens. Her mouth drips and slobbers. Her cheeks rise and fall. Her belly swells like a blown-up bellows. Finally, still hungry, she licks the empty trough clean with her fearsome tongue.

Then the servant goes up to her and gives her a slap on the belly. The cow is startled by Sasha's warm hand and allows herself to be milked.

"Wait, Bashutke, don't go away," Sasha says to me, "you'll soon be drinking a glass of raw milk."

Sasha knows that I cannot bear to hear the squeaking of the cow's teats as the milk gushes out and streams into the pail, like lather, full of foam. It seems to me that the milk tastes of sweat.

"No, Sasha, I have no time. Here comes my teacher. I must go to my lesson."

"Take at least a few drops!"

"Tomorrow I'll take some."

And I run away from her, laughing.

THE BATH

For me the Sabbath begins as early as Thursday toward sunset. In the late evening, mother runs quickly out of the shop as though trying to wrest herself by force from the weekday bustle. While she is still in the shop, I hear her calling out: "Bashke, where are you? We're going to the bathhouse. Sasha, is the linen ready? Hurry, hurry, I have no time!"

The maid quickly wraps up the bundle of linen and ties it with a cord so heavy that the paper bursts. She helps me to put on my coat and galoshes and tightens my hood. I cannot breathe.

"You silly little girl, don't cry," she says, wiping off the tears that well up in my eyes. "It's freezing out—and all I need is that you should catch a cold, God forbid!"

Almost furtively mother and I slip out through the front door of our apartment, as though it were already Saturday and the shop were closed. For mother would be ashamed to go through the shop with the bundle of linen under her arm, although it is wrapped in yellow paper. But the shop is full of men, and besides, who knows but that she might be detained there again. We are in a hurry, chiefly because it is late. Indeed, mother has waited until the last moment to go. The sleigh that is to take us to the bathhouse must be waiting for us at the door. The driver, who is always the same one (he is in fact stationed across from our house) knows that every Thursday evening, almost at the same hour, mother drives to the bathhouse.

The cold, snowy evening at once envelops us in a sheet of frost. In the sleigh, covered with the worn-out fur blanket, I feel through mother's hand as she holds me—lest, God forbid, I should slide down—that she has already forgotten the shop and the bustle that she has just left. She is carried away in the sleigh somewhere into a pure air, as though she were already beginning to tremble in awe of all the holy texts that, God willing, she must recite before the Sabbath comes.

We travel for not so long a time. The driver takes us by a short cut, along the bank of a little river, the Vitbe, near which stands the Jewish bathhouse.

Our sleigh tears silently through the shimmering air. From the high bank of the river trembling little lights are beckoning. This is the glow from Padlo, the little market place, that lies up there on the heights.

I know the market very well, I know its shopkeepers and its little shops, sunk in the earth, and especially the dairy shops. Before going down the stone stairs to the dairy stalls, one had to call on the Lord's help, so wet and slippery were they. And it was cold there as in a grave.

The gray walls dripped water. One single little lamp with a smoked-up glass served to light the whole cellar. Its tiny beam barely reached the mounds of yellow butter, the broad basin that held cream, and even less did it reach the corners where they kept hard, pointed Gomel cheeses, which stuck out like little children's heads.

Only the high scales could be seen clearly. There they were in the middle of the cellar like a throne. Their iron chains swung in the air like two long black braids of hair, and their two brass trays proudly held a tiny bit of merchandise much as if they were supporting Justice herself.

The shopkeepers, in thick, greasy clothes, bustled about in the cellar. With their fingertips sticking out from their mitts they seized pieces of butter, poured pitchers of milk, and tossed curds just as they would snowballs. And while doing all this they yelled as though someone were beating them from behind. They were probably keeping warm in this way. From time to time a coarse word shot through the stuffy cellar. Curses flew out like little tongues of flame, setting ablaze one little stall after another.

"May the cholera take her, for the poisoned food she sells!"

"A curse on my years, if I am lying!"

The stallkeepers would begin to squeal like black mice in their holes. The curses glowed hotter along with the pots of hot coals outside, on which squatted stocky Jewish women peddlers holding bags of roasted beans under their shawls. The shopkeepers reviled one another so warmly and lustily that their dark cellars would grow almost cheerful.

All these cries now accompany us from afar as mother and I drive to the bathhouse. The wind blows a curse at us, tosses it about in the air. The falling snow carries the curse down to the ground. And so we arrive.

"Come back for us, God willing, in a couple of hours," mother says to the driver, although he has been doing this for years.

In the frame vestibule we bump into the ticket seller, wrapped up like a bale of goods. At first she does not stir from her place. One sees only the end of her nose and the tips of her fingers. Next to the tickets there is a glazed apple and a pear. A bit of blue kvass—blue probably from the frost—bubbles in a bottle.

The cashier, as though absorbing our warm breath, slowly undoes her half-frozen mouth and gives us a cold smile.

"It *is* cold to sit here the whole day," she says, beginning to revive. "The wind is blowing from all

sides. A little more of this and one would freeze to death before at last a living being came."

Mother encourages her with a smile and takes from her an apple or a pear for me.

We push at the little door leading to the bath itself. The noise of the latch being raised arouses a couple of naked women resting under their shawls. Like startled flies they jump up from their benches and hum around us.

"Good evening to you, good evening, Alta, my dear! So late! How are you, Alta? Are all the children well? How are you, Bashinke?"

The women touch me from all sides.

"Ah, you're growing up as on yeast—may the evil eye spare you!"

They are warmed up, they have not waited in vain. The shawls like black wings fall from their backs. Before me there flashes the whiteness of their bodies. Everything becomes purer, brighter, all about.

The heat of the anteroom leading to the bath mingles with the cold outside air that has blown in. I can hardly recognize the bath attendants, although they are always the same. I used to think that every Thursday they had grown older, uglier. The younger one, who still smells of her moldy shawl, seizes me at once with her bony hands. "It's cold, isn't it?" she says. "Well, have you unpinned your dress? Have you got another one with you? Well, we'll put it in the box.

Now, hold out your leg—come on!" She urges me as if I were a colt.

And before I have time to look around me, all the buttons of my shoes are unbuttoned, and the shoes with my twisted stockings fly into the black box on which I sit. My buttocks rise and fall with the lid of the box. I have not even had a chance to see what goes on inside the box, into which my belongings are tossed as into a dark pit.

From the frosted window panes, coated over with snow like a pair of blind eyes, a wind blows. I shake from cold. The bath attendant snatches up my sheet and wraps me in it. "Well, wait awhile!" she says. "In a minute you'll be warm! See, we are going to the bath at once."

I feel giddy. She drags me like a bewildered captive straight over to the little door. "Do not fall, Bashinke, God forbid," she says, pulling me with her steely hands. "Walk slowly, it's slippery."

In the doorway to the bath my breath is cut off and I allow myself to be dragged along, half in a faint. A dense cloud veils my eyes. A little tin lamp hangs from its bent hook high above the door. Its chimney, tiny as it is, is still too large for it, and it wobbles in all directions as soon as one touches the door.

I remain glued to the spot. I am afraid to move. The floor is slippery, full of water. Water drips on my feet, drips from the ceiling, from the walls; the whole of the little house is sweating from the heat.

The attendant rushes to the buckets and rinses the slippery bench on which I am supposed to sit. She has no time to say a word to me. Her glistening, scrawny rump twists like the tail of a cat.

Boiling water is poured out, seething. The buckets near me immediately breathe their heat into my face.

The warmth of the bench soothes me and I allow the attendant to put my legs into a bucket of luke-warm water. The woman comes closer to me. Her breasts hang before my eyes like deflated windbags, and her belly, with its skin taut like a drum, comes just under my nose. I am penned up between the buckets and the attendant's belly. I cannot turn, I cannot even think of turning.

Her scratchy fingers gather up my long hair. With one motion she heaps it on my head and begins to rub it with a big cake of Zhukov soap. She pushes the soap back and forth as though she were ironing clothes with it on my head.

Buried under hair, my head whirling, I have no time to think of crying. Smothering my tears, I pull out the bits of acrid soap that cut and bite my eyes. Soap gets into my ears, my mouth. Blindly I dip my fingers into a bucket of cold water beside me.

I get down from the bench only when my hair is rinsed. Long drops of water roll down into my eyes and heal them. I catch my breath, straighten my back; my eyes open.

I hear a creak of the door and on the threshold I

see my whitely nude mother. She is immediately enveloped in the cloud of hot steam. Two attendants hold her at either side. Little tears of sweat drip from their hanging breasts and bellies. A thin little rain of drops, condensed from the steam, suddenly trickles from their hair behind their ears.

Silent and embarrassed, mother stands at the door. Her attendants rush to the buckets, open wide all the taps. They pass steam over the bench for her.

Mother calmly sits down and her body occupies the whole bench. Exhausted from being scrubbed, I hardly see her from where I am. She is ill at ease even before me and lowers her eyes as soon as my glance rests on her hair. Instead of her accustomed thickly curled wig, I see her own short, scraggly hair. Smothered for years without air under the heavy wig, it has thinned out. I become sad, suddenly losing my own strength, and allow myself to be washed without resisting.

My attendant seizes my body, she even lays hands upon my soul. She places me on the bench like a piece of dough and begins to rub and pinch me; she might be trying to knead a challa out of me.

I turn over on my stomach, and she gives me such a whack on my bottom that I jump up.

"Well, what do you say, Bashinke? It's good, isn't it?" says the attendant, suddenly recovering her speech. "Look, how red you have become! It's a pleasure to pinch you!"

[33]

Exhausted, I wait till I am rid of her. Suddenly I am frightened by a flood of water poured on me from behind. For a moment I am engulfed in the stream, the water lifts me and carries me as though I were in a river. This is the attendant rinsing me. From delight and heat, I melt like white wax.

"Oof!" sighs the attendant, wiping her nose with her wet hands. "You're shining just like a little diamond, Bashinke! May this give you health, my child!" She looks at me with her glassy eyes, faded by the water, and quickly wraps me in a warm sheet.

Surely she will at last dry herself off a little. She slowly encircles me with her two arms as if I were her white Sabbath candles that she must bless.

From a distance I watch what is being done to my mother. Surely she has been soaped and rubbed just as I have been, and surely she too has taken delight in the buckets of lukewarm water. But she is not through as quickly as I.

After the scrubbing the older attendant pushes a low stool up to my mother and sits at her feet. She puts a brass candlestick on a little box and lights the piece of candle that is stuck in it. She fans the little flame and begins to complain to mother about her hard life. Her back sinks heavily, as though all her troubles were heaped on it; her drooping head is at mother's feet. "May God have mercy upon us and deliver us from all pain," she says, lifting her eyes from the ground. "So be it, Lord of the Universe!"

She must be trying to forget her own thoughts as she picks at mother's toes. The little flame burns brightly with each blessing she murmurs before cutting the nail. And her heart becomes more serene, it seems, with each blessing. Mother, with lowered eyes, watches what the attendant does to her feet, listens to her patter. Behind the burning candle both are fenced off from the dark bath chamber as within a crown of light. Their heads are close together, their white faces shine in a sort of purification.

Having cleaned mother's toes, the old attendant raises her head and says in a low voice: "Now, Alta, let us go to the mikvah!"

Mother swallows her breath as though the attendant had told a secret. The two rise slowly, straighten their backs, sigh deeply, take a long breath as though preparing to cross the threshold of the holy of holies. Their white shadows vanish in the darkness.

I am afraid to go too. One has to pass a hot chamber where writhing souls lie in torment on long benches. Steaming besoms swing out of the air and lash them and spatter them with drops of hot water. Heavy breathing comes from the benches, as though all of them were being burned on hot coals. The heat presses into my mouth, seizes me by the heart. "This must be a hell for those who have committed many sins!" I think to myself and run after my mother to the mikvah.

I stumble into a black chamber like a prison. On a staircase stands the old attendant. In one hand she holds the burning candle, from her other arm dangles a large white sheet. Mother—I have been so fearful about her—quietly descends the four slippery steps and goes into the water up to her neck. When the old Jewess cries out a blessing, mother is frightened.

[36]

Like one condemned, she holds her nose, closes her eyes, and plunges into the water as though forever—God forbid!

"Ko-o-o-sher!" cries the attendant, with the voice of a prophet.

I am startled as by a thunderclap. Trembling, I wait—surely now lightning will strike from the black ceiling and slay us all on the spot. Or perhaps a deluge will pour from the stone wall and drown us in the dark mikvah.

"Ko-o-o-sher!" the attendant cries out again.

Where is mother? The water does not splash any more. But suddenly the pool splits open and mother's head emerges. She shakes off water as if she were coming up from the very bottom of the sea.

Three times the attendant cries out, and three times mother sinks into the black water.

I am desperately waiting for the moment when the attendant will stop shouting, so that mother will no longer have to disappear in the water. After all, she is tired by now. Water streams down from her hair, from her ears. But she is smiling. Contentment spreads over her whole body. She walks from the water as from a fire, clean and purified. "May it do you good, may it give you health," the attendant says, smiling too.

Her long, thin arms lift the sheet up high. Mother wraps herself in it as in a pair of huge white wings, and smiles on me like a white angel.

[37]

Dressed, all finished with my steaming, I chew my glazed apple, which has long since melted from the heat, and wait for mother. At once she begins to hurry, as though she recalls suddenly that it is a weekday, that the shop is still open. The sanctity and the warmth of the bath slip from her. She is in a hurry to get dressed. The women tell her their last tales of trouble, while one hands her dress to her, the other a shoe. They are probably afraid to leave anything untold, lest they should have to wait until the following Thursday to unburden their hearts. With trembling hands they wrap up our bundle of linen, and they wrap me too like a bundle. Swollen with warmth, I can hardly move.

Mother distributes her tips and listens to the long benedictions with which the women send us off.

"May it give you health, dear Alta! Till next Thursday, if God wills! Keep well, Bashinke! May it do you good!" One woman shouts louder than another, and all of them quickly cover themselves with their shawls.

The door opens as of itself. For a moment we stop on the threshold. What cold! Snow is falling from the black sky. Stars glimmer, and snowflakes. Is it day or night? To my eyes all is white and cold. The driver and his horse have grown into a high white mountain. Are they frozen? "May you have health!" the driver says with a smile.

His wet mustache comes unglued from his mouth.

Little lumps of snow fall from his thick eyebrows. The horse awakens to life and begins to neigh.

"God speed you!" Voices call to us from the door of the bathhouse.

The sleigh starts.

"Hup, hup!" The driver lashes at his thin horse.

Even faster than when she left, mother runs in at the front door and leaves her bundle of linen there. The smell of our apartment and of the shop hits her in the face.

"God alone knows what has gone on here in my absence!" With a look of guilt, she hastens to wash her reddened face and then hurries to the shop.

I am regretting that the warm bath has ended so soon.

SABBATH

From the very morning, Friday begins differently from any other day.

For breakfast, we find on the wide window ledges —in addition to the flat cakes, rolls, and biscuits—a pile of stuffed tsybulnikes. On Friday no dinner is cooked. Instead of hot food, everyone gets a tsybulnik pressed into his hand. Big, thickly filled with fried onions, just as an oven is filled with red coals, the tsybulnik can barely be held in one's hand. The first bite pastes one's mouth shut, and the dough sticks in one's gullet until it is washed down with a glass of cold milk.

"Never mind, you can eat it, you'll have time to get hungry again before supper," Sasha the maid urges me.

On the eve of Sabbath our home is in a bustle all day long. From early morning there is chopping of onions. The kitchen is like a mill. There is fire in the stove. Havah is cooking. Now she bakes challa, then she plucks chickens. Soft feathers pile up in her apron, fly around her head like little chicks fluttering

their wings. Havah chops the mound of peeled onions in a small trough until they are transformed into a pile of wet hash.

Havah's eyes grow wet. It seems that all of us smell of onion. Odors, one sharper than another, pervade the house.

A thick, long fish wriggles in a bucket of water. With widened gills he heavily sucks up the drops. His last strength goes down to his tail, with which he splashes the whole bucket. Having spattered out the water, puffed out his final breath, the fish lies there with gaping mouth. His pointed fins stab one's eyes.

It is as though not one fish but a whole netful has been scattered on the kitchen floor, and each of them wants to snap at us, bite our feet. The cook stands like an executioner before the outstretched pike. His skin still shines with drops of water. She holds the fish by his tail. He slips on the wet board. The cook seizes the cleaver and thrusts it into the plump belly of the fish. Clots of blood fall out. The fish bursts. The cook mercilessly cuts him to pieces. She separates the flesh, removes the skin.

Hashed onions and soaked challa fill the fish with new blood. The stuffed pieces of fish, sprinkled with water, look almost alive. They leap seemingly of their own impulse into the copper pan and are boiled slowly on a small fire until they grow yellow and red. The smell tantalizes us, tickles our noses. It brings us the first taste of Sabbath.

No one stays in his place any longer. The rebbe hurries to the bath with my younger brothers. Sasha busies herself in the dining room, rummages in the cupboards, teases one dawdling brother. "Well, you've had enough tea!" she says. "I must polish the samovar, it will be Sabbath soon!"

"Why do you bother me?" he protests. "You don't even let me drink a glass of tea! A new rebbetzin, of all things!"

Sasha, who has been with us for years, strictly observes the dietary laws about meat and milk foods and keeps the Sabbath like her own Sunday. Without a word, turning her back on my brother, she snatches the samovar from the table, takes under her arm the long tray and the drip bowl full of drops that have trickled down, snatches out of his hand the sugar box and a spoon. Laden like a donkey, she carries all these things to be scrubbed and polished in the kitchen.

On her way she runs into Havah, who walks heavily on her thick legs. With both hands Havah is holding up a large board, as though she had lifted up the floor and were carrying it before her. On the board, which is sprinkled with flour, are two or three plaited, glazed Sabbath loaves, sitting there like empresses. Smaller challas are arrayed around them. All their little heads are decked with thin, twisted braids. At the very edge of the board there is just room for a tiny challa that the cook has plaited for me from a leftover bit of dough. Just out of the oven, all the challas glisten with bronzed cheeks that might almost have got their tan from the sun.

The cook gazes at them and delights in them. She does not want to let them go. "Thanks be to God, the challas turned out well!" she says, smiling and beaming.

The challas slide slowly from the board onto the window ledge. Havah puts a towel under them and covers them with another towel, as though she feared that an evil eye might spoil them. Swelled with heat, the challas are smothered in their own vapors, and cool off slowly.

Father enters, sits down at the table, draws a penknife out of his pocket (how does father happen to have a penknife?) and unfolds a piece of tissue paper. He puts his hands on the table and begins to cut his nails. He cuts them slowly, all round, in half-moons. The nails drop, rattle on the paper. Father wraps them into a little packet and with a blessing on his lips casts them into the stove. He watches how the packet burns and returns to the shop.

"Havah, give me a piece of bread," pleads a Jewish beggar woman, edging into the kitchen.

She is covered with rags; there is one worn-out shawl on her head, another on her shoulders. Her little face is wrinkled like the folds of her dress. Her small forehead is pushed up into the shawl; tangled knots of gray hair droop from under the shawl like dust. Only the eyes glow out from the grayness, like the last pieces of smoldering coal from a heap of ashes. The beggar woman remains standing at the door and screens off all the light from outside. She knows that she is late and she is afraid of the cook. She gives a low sigh.

Havah is fussing with the stove and suddenly she sniffs: she has smelled sour mold. She turns around. "So you've slept well!" she exclaims. "Thank God, here is another one! Who can take care of all of you? What is today, the eve of a new month, or what? All the poor people of the town have been here!"

The beggar woman stands with an air of guilt, lowering her eyes. Havah's voice changes: "You couldn't come earlier? It's almost time to bless the candles now! Take this—it'll get stale anyway before shalesh sudes." Havah grumbles on and sticks half a loaf of bread in the woman's bosom.

"You know," I say to the pauper woman, as though it were a secret, "in front of our shop one of our boys distributes alms."

She gives me a warm look—she has surely been there already, for she comes every Friday—and without a word she quietly leaves the kitchen.

Sasha seizes a pail of water, as if she had to wash the floor clean of the poor beggar woman's presence. First she runs to the dining room, throws off her battered slippers, and stands barefoot in the middle of the room. She looks this way and that, tucks up her skirts, one after the other, hanging them up on herself as it were, swishes her wet rag, and runs all over the floor. Water drips from the pail, from the rag, wets Sasha's white feet.

"Sasha, wait a minute!" I cry to her. "Why do you spout like a fountain? I'll climb on your back and so cross the river of water!"

"Bashke, you crazy child, jump down, at once! You're dirtying my boards all over. Do you hear? If not, I'll give you such a smack on your behind! Oh, what are you doing! Don't tickle me that way! And you're scratching like a cat!" She suddenly straightens her back and I slide down on the wet floor.

"Aha, you've got your punishment? Better come help me push apart the table. You see! It's getting dark already."

We push apart the big dining table and put in the boards. The table grows so long that no matter how much I stretch my arms I cannot reach the other end of it. A white, shining-white tablecloth gives a crackle and runs over the whole table. In a moment, the legs of the table vanish. The ends of the cloth fall down and hang in folds as in a festoon. Sasha runs after me.

"Bashutke, where are you?" she calls. "Here, hang up the towels, each on its nail."

"The napkins are still here—what shall I do with them?" I ask.

"Put one on father's Sabbath bread."

I go to father's place and cover the Sabbath bread as one covers a bride with a veil.

At the other end of the table mother's great five-branched silver candlestick is already in its place. Probably to make a lucky number, two single-branched candlesticks are added. In all the seven sockets long white candles are swaying. Beside mother's candlestick my own little candlestick seems hardly able to stand on its short legs. Father gave it to me as a gift. Its scratched silver is carved like a transparent cobweb. The little socket has a shield piece under it, where later my candle will die drop by drop.

The table, like a white dream palace, stands so calm, it might be awaiting something. Suddenly the fringes of the tablecloth begin to flutter. From somewhere a distant noise reaches me. I hear the shutters of the shop falling. The unrolling metal screeches. Thank God, the shop is being closed at last! I make out the voices of the employees, hastening home. "Go now, leave everything! You might miss your streetcar!" This is mother speeding the cashier, who lives at the edge of the town and is in the habit of lingering in the shop longer than anyone else.

Now father comes in. I stand waiting for him as for a guest. "Bashke, don't you know where I can find a clean collar and a pair of cuffs?" he asks.

"Here, father, they're on the dressing table."

Father passes by the mirror, turns away his head; he has seen his face in the mirror.

"What a nuisance! Why are the buttonholes ironed in so tightly that there's no way of pushing a button through?" Father sweats and chokes in getting on his fresh collar.

"Father, do you want me to ask Sasha for another collar?"

"Who has time for that? We must soon go to shul."

Sasha brings in the samovar, lights the lamp. The polished samovar boils and bubbles like a locomotive. The hanging lamp spatters fire. It is now warm and light all around. Father sits at the table quietly taking sweet tea with jam.

The last to leave the shop is mother. She tries all the doors once more to see that they are locked. Now I hear her pattering steps. Now she shuts the metal door of the rear shop. Now her dress rustles. Now her soft shoes slip into the dining room. In the doorway she halts for a moment: the white table with the silver candlesticks dazzles her eyes. At once she begins to hurry. She quickly washes her face and hands, puts on a clean lace collar that she always wears on this night, and approaches the candlesticks like a quite new mother. With a match in her hand she lights one candle after another. All the seven candles begin to quiver. The flames blaze into mother's face. As though an enchantment were falling upon her, she lowers her eyes. Slowly, three times in succession, she encircles the candles with both her arms; she seems to be taking them into her heart. And with the candles her weekday worries melt away.

She blesses the candles. She whispers quiet benedictions through her fingers and they add heat to the flames. Mother's hands over the candles shine like the tablets of the decalogue over the holy ark.

I push closer to her. I want to get behind her blessing hands myself. I seek her face. I want to look into her eyes. They are concealed behind her spread-out fingers.

I light my little candle by mother's candle. Like her, I raise my hands and through them, as through a gate, I murmur into my little candle flame the words of benediction that I catch from my mother.

My candle, just lighted, is already dripping. My hands circle it to stop its tears.

I hear mother in her benedictions mention now one name, now another. She names father, the children, her own father and mother. Now my name too has fallen into the flame of the candles. My throat becomes hot.

"May the Highest One give them his blessing!" concludes mother, dropping her hands at last.

"Amen," I say in a choking voice, behind my fingers.

"Good shabbes!" mother calls out loudly. Her face, all opened, looks purified, I think that it has absorbed the illumination of the Sabbath candles.

[49]

"Good shabbes!" answers father from the other end of the table and rises to go to shul.

"Good shabbes!" cries the cook from the kitchen. Havah likewise has taken her two brass candlesticks from the shelf and has stuck a couple of short candles in them. The well-used table is covered with a small white tablecloth—the toilworn kitchen is unrecognizable. The white tablecloth and the two white candles have given it rest.

Every kitchen object is put away or hung up in its place. Even the stove has been sealed with a black sheet of metal. The front part of the stove is cleared of pots and pans. The walls are whiter, they have dried of their sweat. Every corner is swept clean, scrubbed. It is Sabbath.

Havah sits at the table; she does not know what to do with her empty hands. She is suddenly seized with sadness. She feels like being alone, in order to be something of a mistress at least for a little while. "Sasha, go out for a moment," she says to the gentile maid, pointing with her eyes to the door.

Havah, left alone, lights the candles. She has lived for many years with strangers, has grown up among them; she recalls that she too once had a father, a mother, her own home.

"Baruch ha-Shem, blessed be thy Name. God did not want to bless me with my own household—I must have sinned." She drops a tear. Her eyes seem to merge with the candlelight. "But praise be to the Highest that I am living with respectable people, in a Jewish household. After all, we are Jews. Ah!"—and she sighs—"I had a prayer book somewhere. Where have I put it? Without a holy word, night and day with the shikse, I might become benighted." She finds her grease-stained prayer book, opens it, and blesses her candles aloud.

Everyone has gone to shul. Mother and I are alone at home. The white table with the candles is illumined for us alone. It seems to me that the sky too has been warmed by the candles and is peeping in at the window. Mother is sitting under the twinkling overhead lamp and is praying quietly. Her benedictions are a murmur; occasionally a candle gives a sigh. My own little candle has almost completely burned down. I move closer to the wall and begin to say the Silent Prayer.

The wall breathes, breathes as if it were alive. I want to grow into it. I am afraid to touch it, even with the prayer book in my hand. Now voices resound in the entrance hall. There are my brothers, who have come back from shul. They are bustling at the door, outshouting one another. "Well, how did you like the cantor? He was in a hurry—you'd have thought the house was on fire!"

"And have you at least said the whole of the Silent Prayer?"

"I? I stood near Uncle Berel—and he began to spit."

[51]

"Ah, you're an uncouth fellow, Israel! Better help me to pull out my sleeve, the lining has suddenly got twisted up like a Turkish beigel."

"Come, come, it's your brain that's twisted!"

They throw their coats at each other.

Mendel dreams, off at one side: "If I am called tomorrow to the scroll of the Law—"

"Then you'd shake like a broom," Abrashke finishes for him.

"Sh-sh!" the rebbe hurls at them as he enters our apartment. "All you can do is make mock of everything! At least say 'Good shabbes,' shkutsim!"

The rebbe grumbles in a low tone, calmly; his weekday fever seems to be suspended in honor of the Sabbath.

Why do they, my brothers, always come back from shul so excited? They have to be driven to go there—"It's late, go to shul!" After they are back, they never stop laughing. They have enough stories for the whole week. What goes on there in shul? And what does father do there, staying such a long time? He always comes back last. Probably he is disturbed by the men who pray in loud tones. And so father stands up to say the Silent Prayer when everyone else is preparing to go home. Even on Friday nights he stays in shul for a long time. After everyone has left, it is quiet there—only a couple of flies hum around the burning lamps.

Father, alone in his place at the east wall, sways from side to side, like the tree in the yard of the shul, near the window. He prays in a low voice, with closed eyes; he appears detached from the world. His sentences are whispered, then they take wing around him. From a distance the shames watches him. The shames is a thin little man, thin against the thick books piled up on the little table near him.

The shames himself has finished his prayers long before. He finishes first, in order that his betters need not wait for him. And so he sits silent as the wall and waits for father. When father rocks himself, the shames too rocks in his corner. When father utters a groan, the shames sighs too. When the shames hears father shuffling his feet, he gets up at once. When father moves away from the wall, the shames jumps up from his bench. "Good shabbes, good shabbes, Reb Shmul Noah!" he exclaims, running toward him, pleased that father has finished the Silent Prayer and that he himself will be able to take rest for a while.

"Good shabbes!" father answers, still dreamily, and spits out toward all three sides. The shames helps him to put on his coat.

"Reb Shmul Noah," the shames says in a low voice, "in the courtyard there are still a couple of soldiers, sons of respectable Jews, among strangers!"

"What are you saying?" Father comes to life. "Go quickly and tell them not to go away, let them come with me. A Jewish child without the Sabbath supper! God forbid!"

Father is embarrassed over getting home late.

"Good shabbes!" he says, entering the room hurriedly. "Alta, I've brought some decent, respectable Jews. Ask them to supper." He calls to mother and points to the two soldiers, who have shyly remained standing in the doorway.

My brothers fall silent and gaze at the guests. Abrashke cannot restrain himself and jumps toward them. The glittering military buttons dazzle his eyes. He cannot sit still, he must touch each thing separately.

"Let me put on your belt, will you? And where is your gun?"

My brothers drag the soldiers to their end of the table. Father goes to wash his hands. Three times he pours water from the heavy copper jug on each hand separately, and slowly he wipes each finger. After him my brothers rush to the washstand. Each tries to wrest from the other the bit of water remaining in the jug after father has finished. They tear the towel from each other's hands.

The chairs are pushed away, pushed back. Each stays in his place by some compulsion.

"Sh-shah!" father cries out. "What's that quarreling on the Sabbath? You ought to be ashamed, before strangers! Well, enough—kiddush!" He points to the goblet filled with wine.

Everyone rises. There is silence. The cook places herself in the doorway. Father waits awhile, as though gathering strength. The silver goblet, all engraved with black little flowers, sways like a full bucket in his hand. The wine spills over his fingers, spatters the white tablecloth. Father pushes the goblet more firmly into his hand and now holds it with all five fingers. He sways once to one side, then to the other. He begins the kiddush. With closed eyes father whispers the benedictions; they might be coming out of the goblet. His wide forehead is wrinkled up. His voice changes to a tune that becomes infused with the wine. And like the tune the wine grows richer, more glowing. The tune rocks us too as we stand silently.

"Amen!" Father raises the goblet to his mouth and, with his eyes still lowered, drinks off a little of the wine.

"Amen!" all of us answer in one voice.

"Amen!" echoes the cook from the door and rushes back to the kitchen.

Mother silently swallows a few drops of wine and whispers: "We have lived to see the Sabbath, all of us are in good health. Thanks be to the Highest!"

"Say a blessing, Bashinke!" She suddenly remembers and gives me a sip from the goblet.

The wine stings my mouth.

I sit in my corner as usual between father and mother. Their breath blows into my face. Occasionally father's beard strokes my shoulder. A drop of wine has remained hanging on his mustache, it is as though the kiddush cup with its wine had pressed the blood to his lips.

"Do you want to say kiddush?" Father offers the cup to the elder soldier, and the drop of wine from his mustache falls on me.

"No, thank you!" The shy guest blushes and clears his throat.

"Well, now the blessing on the bread!" Father says the benediction over the loaves and cuts them into slices.

A tableful of hands stretch out toward father. Then suddenly everyone's eyes are fixed on the maid entering the room. There is a whiff of onion and pepper.

Sasha, her face flushed, because everyone is waiting for her, slowly carries to mother the platter of fish. Like a boat it sways in her hands. The pieces of fish are piled on so thickly that it is hard to turn them over. One portion jostles another, clings to the other. The pieces stand frozen in the pond of jellied sauce that moistens them underneath.

"Mother, give me the round piece, the one near the edge there!"

Mother pries up one piece of fish after another, places them on the plates. Her hand does not come to rest. The heads around the table bend over the plates. There is chewing, smacking. On some plates the fishbones begin to appear. And mother keeps on dealing out portions. Suddenly father wipes his mouth and asks the soldiers: "Where are you from? Have you parents? What is their trade?"

The soldiers raise their bent heads—they are busy picking the bones—then look frightened as though they had been caught unawares. They stammer with their mouths full.

My brothers begin: "Listen, what are you told to do in the barracks? Are your officers kind to you? Aren't you beaten? And where do you sleep? Can you hold a gun?"

The two soldiers, being fired at from all sides, push away their plates. They do not know what to do, whom to answer first, whether or not to resume eating in order to avoid having the others wait for them.

"Children, let the guests alone! Why do you set upon them like that? This way we won't get through supper before midnight!"

A large bowl of soup is brought in. Steam mounts from it. It holds golden chicken soup; red veins of saffron swim in it, kernels of rice drift about in it, and two white boiled chickens lie there lifelike.

"Mother, may I have the gizzard?" Abrashke jumps up first.

Mother gives him a look: "Well, this one doesn't forget himself!" She turns to me. "Here, my child, take a leg. And here is some more tsimes. You like sweet tsimes, don't you?"

Red, flaming little carrots smile at me from my plate.

"And who wants a wing?"

The two wings stretch out from mother's hands—a bird ready to fly away. Mother divides the chicken in pieces. One gets a neck, another a wing. She has hardly time to take her own portion.

All of us are foundered. Our eyelids are sticking together. The tablecloth is full of stains. The feast dies out together with the candles.

Saturday after dinner. Our house is asleep. Only Havah the cook is awake. All week long she waits for the Sabbath, and when it comes she thinks that it will not end, that she will have time to go over all her dresses, boast of the gifts she has received, change clothes, and go out for a walk, and walk without ceasing. She opens her chest and vanishes in it. She airs out, fingers, rummages in the pile of clothes as in a pile of her years.

"You see, I received this gift last Passover. The hat belonged to my former mistress, who—"

"You've dawdled enough! Everyone else has long been walking in the street!" The gentile maid makes fun of her.

"Can I go out this way? What shall I wear?"

All furbished up as for a wedding—she has become three times as fat—the cook can hardly stand on her legs. Her new shoes pinch. But she stands there, all billowed up, already feeling the eyes of the people in the street upon her.

"Tell me, Sasha, will anyone recognize that I'm a servant?"

She brandishes the small tin mirror, touches herself all over. "Here, look—it's real silk!"

She pulls up her dress, straightens her hat, which is all stuck over with flowers, and walks slowly across the threshold, as though beyond it she would instantly enter a new world.

Now the whole street will stare at her. Everyone will turn around to have a look at her dress, her hat, and who knows—perhaps this Sabbath she will finally meet the man destined to be her husband. She gives herself a shake as she stands and says to the gentile maid in the tone of a mistress: "Sasha, when the masters get up, serve them the jug of tea."

A few hours later she returns from her walk, more tired than she would be from a whole week of work. The house is now full of people who have come for the third meal. They hum the Rabbi's Song. One explains to another: "What is the text? The rabbi has said—"

It seems that they are having a dispute. When they are served cold fried fish, they cool off at once.

Sunset is approaching. Father looks out of the window, finds the first little star that has risen in the blue sky with the new moon. He goes out. Big father grows quite little under the heavenly moonlight. I trail after him: "Father, will you light the havdalah?"

We return to the house. I hold the wax candle. It is

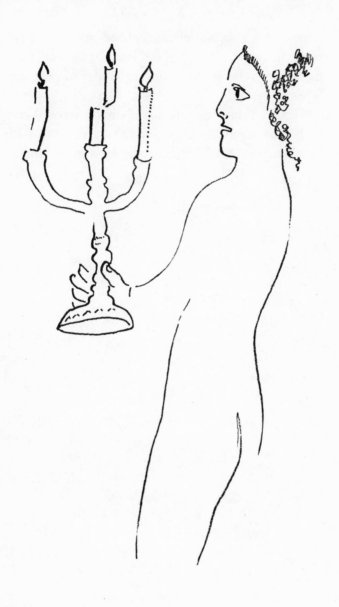

twisted like a heavy chain, imbued with weekday sweat. Its flame is heavy and thick. Father snuffs out the candle in the wine splashes at the edge of the table.

"Gute woch!"

"Gute woch—may you have a good week!" says mother pensively. Her face is already covered with weekday grayness. "May it really be a good week!"

THE MELAMMED

THE old teacher who comes to give us lessons sidles through the yard like a shadow. My heart sinks at once.

Small, short, he almost presses himself into the wall, as though he feared that he might touch someone. His worn-out coat, of a black-green color, hardly wraps around his narrow shoulders. His little plucked goatee droops down.

"Well, Bashinke?" He squeezes out a smile. "Have you memorized the alphabet? Go call Abramele. Today we'll study well, won't we?"

"Abrashke, Abrashke, the teacher has come!" I run into the apartment, calling.

But my brother probably sighted the teacher before I did. He whispers to me from the little room into which he locks himself each time the lesson hour comes: "Go pour a glass of tea with jam in the meantime."

"But you'll come, won't you?" I whisper through the crack in the door. "I can't stay alone with the teacher for the whole time."

"Go, get away from here. I'll come right away. Tell him I have a tummy-ache."

The teacher goes to the table.

"Ugh!" he inhales, sighs, blows his nose, wipes his spectacles, and takes snuff. Perked up, he opens the book that he always carries with him.

"Well, where are you, children?" He turns his head but does not remove his finger from the line.

"Here I am, teacher! Here is a glass of tea. Do you want it, teacher?" I put a glass of hot tea with jam near the book.

The vapor of the tea clouds his spectacles. The sweet fragrance of cherry juice titillates his nose.

The teacher sips a few drops, warms up. He does not put the glass back until he has finished drinking the tea.

"Teacher, do you want another glass?" I do not wait for an answer and run away with the glass in my hand.

"Where is Abramele? Is he at home?" And the teacher begs me not to bring him any more tea.

"Yes, teacher, I am going to call him. He said he'd come right away."

"Abrashke!" I knock at his door. "The teacher is waiting for you. Come out!"

"Have you given him tea? And jam?"

"Of course—a couple of glasses, even. He is already sick from the jam. I'm scared. Come out, at least for a minute!"

"Is it my fault? I can't come out. Now I've really got a tummy-ache."

I know that Abrashke is lying. Nothing is wrong with him. He only wants to dawdle there through the lesson time.

I return to the teacher. He sits embarrassed by his empty glass.

"Teacher, perhaps you'd like another glass of tea? I've just had new hot coals added under the samovar." And before he can collect himself, I snatch the glass from his hand.

I am ashamed to put it on the table. I am ashamed to look the teacher in the eye. The steam of the hot tea blows straight up into his face. His eyes begin to blink.

Suddenly I am overcome by fear that the old man will faint on the spot from the heat. Even now he sits as though he had no strength, his eyes closed, his head drooping.

I look at the teacher, and do not recognize him—he has suddenly become very old.

Of his whole body hidden behind the table, only his little head with the goatee can be seen. But now I notice that his face is tired out, that his neck is thin. He is yellow, from the yellow page in the book that has remained lying open on the table. His mustache and the tips of his fingers are yellow, too, worn from pinching snuff.

Is he really so old? Does his coat too smell of old-ness?

"Perhaps," I think to myself, "the teacher won't be able to get home by himself. Perhaps we should ask his relatives to come for him. Does anyone know where the teacher lives? Has he children? Are they as bad as we are? He has no one." And my heart begins to pound—the teacher is alone in the world, like a stone.

I am glad that the old man is asleep, that he does not see how I have become red in the face. I fancy that he has sunk into sleep not because of all the glasses of sweetened tea, but from grief because we do not want to study with him. He is such a quiet man, he wants to teach us at least the alphabet, bring us, as he says, to a page of the Bible.

Then why is he afraid to be firm with us? It would be better if he shouted at us! After all, we are not the parents—his employers, as he says.

We are wicked! Only when the teacher is asleep do we pity him!

I feel like saying to him that beginning today (I can swear it by anything) I will study well, that I will no longer bring him so many glasses of tea. I am afraid. My whispering is too noisy—I might waken the teacher from his sleep. So I remain sitting quietly in my place.

"Oh!" I remind myself. "Abrashke might just at this moment jump out of his little room and waken the teacher! Let the old man at least take a good nap in our house! He probably studies the Torah at night and does not sleep enough."

Suddenly through the open window I catch the smell of sweet chocolate boiling. The odor is so strong that I glance at the teacher to see whether it has not wakened him. The aroma is like a sweet cloud around my head. It pricks my tongue, tickles my nose. I am getting drunk.

I am annoyed to think that I am not in the courtyard just now. I know that the chocolate is boiling in the kitchen of the confectionery, the Jean Albert, which is situated under our own kitchen. They use the chocolate for icing the cakes they bake.

If I could only show myself now, the bakers would be calling me over to them. They would be giving me the big wooden ladle with which they stir the chocolate, to let me lick it. The old baker of whom I am so afraid outside in the courtyard is sweeter when he is inside his warm kitchen than the cakes that he shapes so skillfully. He smiles with those black teeth of his that are worn out from eating sugar. His white apron is stained, smeared with all the creams with which he covers the cakes.

I see the baker raising to his mouth a twisted, long horn. From the horn a colored dense cream blows out, and on the cake waiting under it a red flower is turned out here, a green leaf there.

The baker puffs on another horn, and a little angel with wings jumps onto the very top of the cake. He takes a wooden spatula in his hand and smooths out the little angel, smooths the cake on all sides. Sweet crumbs drop from it.

The baker knows that I look upon him as a magician.

"Beautiful, isn't it?" He smiles. "Do you want the scraps?"

I am waiting for the scraps. He crams fistfuls of sweet crumbs into my hands.

I open my hand—there is nothing in it. I look about —the teacher is asleep.

Ah, when will he finish sleeping? This way I'll miss the sweet crumbs. It will be late, and I won't be able to go to the confectioner's dark kitchen.

Shall I run out for a while? And what if the teacher should suddenly wake up?

"Sh-sh-sh!" I hear a swish suddenly, like the whistling of a wind. What is that? Is it not just the teacher whistling through his nose? I look out of the window. I almost fall flat. From above, from the photographer's apartment, there is a downpour of many little white leaves.

Crumpled, they fly, turn over, fall down to the stairs, over the courtyard; they might be white little doves fluttering down there. I stretch out my hands, trying to snatch at one of the little pieces of paper. I know that they are pictures that the photographer is throwing out. Yellow, pale, speckled—in some the eye is pierced, in others the cheeks are broken; one can hardly make out a whole person on any of them.

There sits a girl with goggling eyes, as though she were choking in the high collar that peaks up into her ears. There stands a soldier with long mustaches, with frightened eyes—he may be seeing a general from afar off, scolding him.

A little cardboard falls into my hand. I look at it. Thank God I've caught it!

It has a naked baby lying on a piece of sheet. Although the baby is as plump as a piglet, it would have broken its little head if it had fallen on the ground.

"Play with me! Smile at me!" I fancy that the baby begins to smile.

And now a picture crammed with people falls into my hand. How could the photographer have the heart to throw them out all together?

A whole family in a single picture—a grandfather and a grandmother, and another grandmother, an uncle and an aunt, a father and mother, sons and daughters, married folk and little girls, tiny children. There were not enough chairs to seat them all. So those who are standing up behind are angry. Children are sitting on the floor.

Once I looked and looked at such groups and could not restrain myself. I went to ask mother why we too should not have our pictures taken all together.

"After all, the photographer is living in our house," I said. "And we could see ourselves on the display panel that hangs across from our shop."

Mother gave me a look. "Are you crazy," she exclaimed, "out of your mind? Have you nothing else to think about? Out of a blue sky, we are to have our pictures taken, like the shikses with their soldier boys?"

Why does mother shout like that? Wasn't grandfather photographed once? True, he had to be hoodwinked: he was told, while he was standing quietly behind the counter, that he must not move from the spot, that the shop was being measured. Why then shouldn't the photographer in our house be asked to measure our shop, and while this is being done take a picture of all of us?

"Bashke!" Finally Abrashke runs out of his little room with a shout. "Has the teacher gone?"

"S-sss!" And I make signs to him with my hands, in fright. "Stop yelling—the teacher is asleep!"

But Abrashke's cry has wakened the teacher. Thank God, after his nap he seems fresher.

He collects himself at once, notices us, and turns to his book, as though he had not slept at all.

"Well, children, where are we? Repeat after me— aleph, beth."

"Aleph, beth, gimel, daleth," I say loudly, happy that the teacher finds nothing to reproach us about.

"Heh, vav!" Abrashke tries to outshout me.

For the first time we recite the alphabet from beginning to end.

The old man smiles with pleasure. "Aren't you

[71]

tired, children?" he asks. "You've studied well today, eh? Perhaps it's enough for today? Eh?"

The teacher puts on his worn coat and quietly goes out of the room.

ROSH HA-SHANAH

THE Fearful Days have come, and our whole house is in an uproar. Each holiday brings with it its own savor, each is steeped in its own atmosphere. A clear, joyful, purified air, as after a rain—this is the air of Rosh ha-Shanah.

After the black nights of the Selichot prayers a bright, sunny day dawns for the New Year. The week of Selichot is the most restless week. Father wakes up in the middle of the night, rouses my brothers, and all of them dress quietly and go off like thieves slinking through the door.

What are they looking for in the cold, in the dark streets? It is so warm in bed! And what if they don't come back at all—how mother and I would weep and weep! I am almost beginning to cry even now, and I wrap myself closer in my blankets.

In the morning when father drinks his tea his face is pale and fagged. But the bustle of the holiday eve dispels everyone's weariness.

The shop is closed at an early hour. Everybody makes ready to go to shul. There are more preparations than ever before, as if it were the first time they were going there. Each one puts on something new—one a fresh, light-colored hat, another a new necktie, still another a new garment.

Mother dons a white silken blouse; she seems refurbished, she has a new soul, and she is eager to go to shul.

One of my elder brothers opens the thick prayer book for her and creases down the pages from which she must pray. They are marked with notations made by grandfather's hand many years ago: "Say this."

Mother recognizes the lines over which she wept last year. A trembling comes over her and her eyes dim with tears. She is in a hurry to go to shul to weep over the words, as if she were reading them for the first time.

A stack of books has been prepared for her. She wraps them in a large kerchief and takes them all with her. Must she not pray for a good year for the whole family?

As for father's books and talis, the shames came to fetch them to the shul during the day.

I remain behind, alone. The house is empty, and I too feel emptied. The old year, like a thing forlorn, drags itself away somewhere outside. The coming year must be a clear one, a bright one. I want to sleep through the night as quickly as possible.

On the following day in the morning I too go to shul. I too wear new garments from tip to toe. The

sun is shining, the air is clear and alive. My new shoes
give a dry tap. I walk faster. The New Year must be
already arrived in shul. The shofar must be sounding
there; even now it echoes in my ears. I fancy that the
sky itself has come down lower and hurries to shul
together with me. I run to the women's section, I push
open the door. A whiff of heat comes from in there,
as from an oven. The heavy air stifles my breath. The
shul is packed full. The high lecterns are piled with
books. Old women sit bent, sunk in their chairs. Girls
stand almost on the heads of the grandmothers. Children tumble underfoot.

I want to elbow my way to mother. But she is sitting so far off, all the way up at the front, next to the window that opens into the men's section. As soon as I try to move, a woman turns around to me, a weeping face gives me an angry look.

"Oh! Oh!" She breathes wrath at me.

I am pushed from behind; I am suddenly freed, and thrown to the handrail.

My mother signals to me with her eyes. She is glad that I am near her. But where is the shofar? Where is the New Year?

I look at the walls of the men's section. The ark of the Torah is closed, its curtain drawn. Silently and calmly the two embroidered lions guard it. The congregation is in a tumult, as though busy with something else. Have I come too early or too late?

Suddenly from under a talis a hand holding a shofar stretches out and remains suspended in the air. The shofar blares out; everyone is awakened. They are all very still. They wait. The shofar gives another blast. The sound is chopped off, as though the horn were out of breath.

People exchange glances. The shofar trumpets hoarsely. A murmur ripples through the shul.

What manner of shofar blowing is that? He lacks strength. Perhaps another man should be called up.

And then suddenly, as though the trumpet blower had pushed out the evil spirit that was clogging the shofar, there comes a pure, long sound. Like a summons it runs through the whole shul, sounding into every corner. The congregation is relieved: one gives a sigh, another nods his head. The sound rises upward. The walls are touched by it. It reaches me and my handrail. It throbs up to the ceiling, pushes the thick air, fills every empty space. It booms into my ears, my mouth, I even feel an ache in my stomach. When will the shofar finish, trumpeting? What does the New Year want of us?

I recall all my sins. God knows what will happen to me: so much has accumulated during the year!

I can hardly wait for afternoon. I am eager to go with mother to the rite of tashlich, to shake off all my sins, cast them into our big river. Other women and men are on their way. All of them walk down the little street that leads to the river bank. All of them are dressed in black; they might be going, God forbid, to a funeral. The air is sharp. From the high river bank, from the big city park, a wind is blowing; leaves are falling, yellow, red-yellow, like butterflies; they whirl in the air, turn over, scatter on the ground. Do our sins fly in the same way? The leaves rustle, stick to my shoes. I drag them along. Having them, it is less fearsome to go through the tashlich.

"Why do you stop all the time?" Mother pulls me by the hand. "Let the leaves alone!"

Soon everyone stops. The street seems suddenly to end; the deep, cool waters seem to be flowing up to our feet.

[77]

On the river bank dark clusters of people have gathered. The men, with their heads thrust out and their beards swaying, bend down to the water, as though they wanted to see the very bottom. Suddenly they turn their pockets inside out; little crumbs, scraps, detach themselves from the linings. The men recite a prayer aloud and throw their crumbs, together with the sins, into the water. But how shall I shake off my sins? I have no crumbs in my pockets— I do not even have pockets.

I stand next to mother, shivering from the cold wind that lifts our skirts. Mother tells me the ritual words that I have to say, and the prayers together with the sins fall from my mouth straight into the water. I fancy that the river is swollen with all our sins, and it rolls along with its waters suddenly turned black.

My burden eased away, I return home. Mother at once sits down to read psalms. She wants still to make use of the day to obtain something more from God. A humming fills the dark room. The air becomes clouded, like mother's spectacles. Mother is weeping, silently shaking her head.

What shall I do?

I fancy that from the closely printed lines of the psalms our grandfathers and grandmothers come gently out to us. Their shadows sway, they draw themselves out like threads, encircle me. I am afraid to turn around. Perhaps someone is standing at my back and wants to seize me in his arms?

"Mother!" I cannot contain myself, I shake her by
the sleeve.

She raises her head, blows her nose, and ceases
weeping. She kisses the psalter and closes it.

"Bashke," she says, "I'm going to shul. We'll be
back soon, all of us. Will you set the table, my child?"

"Mother, is it for the shehecheyanu?"

As she goes out I open the cupboards. I drag out
the tall paper bags filled with fruit and spread all of it

out on the table. As in a great garden, thick green melons roll on the table. Beside them lie clusters of grapes, white and red. Big, juicy pears have turned over on their little heads. There are sweet yellow apples that have a golden gleam—they look as if they had been dipped in honey. Plums, dark red, scatter all over the table.

Over what shall we offer the benediction of first fruits? Haven't we eaten of all these things all year long?

I notice that from another bag there protrudes, like a fir tree, a pineapple, a new, unfamiliar fruit.

"Sasha, do you know where pineapples grow?"

"Who knows?" She spreads her hands. "I've got other things to think about!"

No one knows whence the pineapple comes. With its scaly skin it looks like a strange fish. But its tail stands up at the top like an opened fan. I touch its stuffed belly, and it trembles from top to bottom. It is not a casual matter to touch the pineapple; it behaves somewhat like an emperor. I reserve the center of the table for it.

Sasha slices it pitilessly. The pineapple groans under her sharp knife like a live fish. Its juice, like white blood, trickles onto my fingers. I lick them. It is a tart-sweet taste.

Is this the taste of the New Year?

"Dear God," I whisper hurriedly, "before they all come back from shul, give a thought to us! Father and mother pray Thee all day long in shul to grant them a good year. And father always thinks of Thee. And mother remembers thy Name at every step! Thou knowest how toilworn they are, how care-ridden. Dear God, Thou canst do everything! Make it so that we have a sweet, good year!"

I quickly sprinkle powdered sugar on the pine-apple.

"Gut yom-tov! Gut yom-tov!" My brothers run in, trying to outshout one another.

They are followed immediately by father and mother, who look pale and tired.

"May you be inscribed for a happy year!"

My heart leaps up. I imagine that God himself is speaking through their mouths.

DAY OF ATONEMENT

A QUITE different air, heavy and thick, pervades the night of Yom Kippur.

All the shops are long closed. Their black shutters are locked as though forever. The sky too is black, as if God himself—heaven forbid—had deserted it. It is terrifying to walk in the streets. Perhaps God metes out punishment instantly, and one will sprain an ankle. I shudder at hearing laughter somewhere in the distance. The goyim are not afraid at all. They laugh even on the Day of Atonement.

My head is still throbbing with the clamor that came from father's white kapporeh rooster.

A black-garbed, scrawny-looking shochet slunk into our courtyard late in the evening. From the folds of his coat a long knife flashed. He chased father's cock; the cock shrieked, shaking the courtyard with his din. Other cocks ran after him with excited cries.

The cook seized a cock by the leg, but the cock wrenched himself free. The courtyard was littered with feathers.

It sounded like a thousand gongs clanging for a fire: the courtyard re-echoed with the crowing of the cocks, with their embattled uproar. But gradually they spent their strength. The yard grew quieter and quieter.

Mother's and my own white chicken hid in a hole in their fear. One could only hear them clucking low and crying.

The cook caught both chickens at the same time and put them at the shochet's feet. Blood poured over the whole balcony. When I came to myself, all the cocks and hens lay on the ground. From their necks ran threads of blood. Blood had spattered their white feathers. They were left to cool off in the dark night.

I remember how my little chicken quivered in my hands when I held it upraised for the rite. I too was quivering. My finger recoiled at once when I touched the chicken's warm belly. The chicken uttered a shriek, and tried to fly over my head, like a little white angel.

I raised my eyes from the prayer book, I wanted to look at the chicken. It cried and clucked as though begging for mercy of me. I did not hear the passages that I was to repeat. And I was suddenly seized by fear that the chicken, as I held it up high, might befoul my head.

Mother is calling me. From a distance I see her eyes gleaming, her hands moving quietly as though preparing to embrace someone. She tells me to hold the skeins of thread before the large wax candles that will burn in the shul at the cantor's reading stand. She pulls out the first thread.

"For my beloved husband, for Shmul Noah—may he be healthy and live to his hundred-and-twentieth year." She draws out the thread, slowly weaves a benediction into it, sprinkles it with her tears, and passes a big piece of wax over it, as though trying to rub it full of good wishes.

"Hold fast to the end of the thread, Bashke," mother says to me.

"For my dear son, for Itchke—may he be healthy and live in happiness and joy till his hundred-and-twentieth year!" She draws out the second thread and rubs it too with wax.

"For my oldest daughter, for Hannah."

Names are slowly intoned, threads are drawn, now yellow with wax and tears. I can hardly hold all the ends that remain free of wax. They slip from the tips of my fingers. I hold them with all my strength.

Mother prays a long time for each child, each relative. I no longer know what she is saying. With every name a tear drops on the thread and at once is imbedded in the wax like a little pearl. One heavy candle is now ready. Mother tackles the others.

"May all of us live long. For my deceased father, Baruch Aaron Raishkes—may he rest forever in paradise. My father, pray well for us, for me and my husband and my little children. Entreat from God good health and good fortune for all of us." Now mother weeps aloud. She almost cannot see the threads shaking in her hands.

"May all of us live long. For my deceased mother, Aige—may she pray well for us. My mother, do not forsake your only daughter, Alta," mother prays over the thread she has drawn out. Apparently she would like to linger with her mother as long as possible; she moves the wax slowly and does not let the thread go from her hands.

"May all of us live long. For my deceased little son, Benjamin." Mother begins to weep again.

At this point I can check myself no longer. I weep too over my little brother who was one year old when he died and whom I never saw.

Mother glances at me through her tears, catches her breath, and blows her nose. The skein of threads grows thicker and thicker. Dead relatives, members of closely and distantly connected families, come as on a visit to us. For each one mother sheds a tear; it is like sending a greeting to every one of them. I no longer hear their names; I might be walking around an unfamiliar graveyard. I see only stones, I see only threads. I am even filled with fear at the thought of how many dead relatives have been drawn forth and entwined among mother's threads. Will we, the living, burn in the same way, like the souls of the dead?

I am glad when at last the shames, who is waiting

for the candles, carries them to the shul. Exhausted, I go to bed.

Next day we are prompted from early morning on. We are given a special snack, in order to fortify us before the fast, and to give us opportunity to say another prayer. We are trying to do good deeds. My brothers apologize to one another.

"Abrashke, you're not angry with me?" I rush to my brother—I recall that I have not always done things he wanted me to do.

Mother goes down to the courtyard. There is a neighbor with whom she has quarreled. She begs him earnestly to forgive her.

My brothers change clothes, make ready to go to shul. They almost do not speak. They do not even jostle one another. They seem to have been seized with awe.

They wait at some distance while mother slowly blesses her candles. Then they come first to father, next to mother, wishing them both a good year. My parents place their hands on each of them and speak a blessing upon each head. Even the grown sons and daughters look like little children under the outspread hands of their parents. I, the youngest, go to them last. Father, with lowered eyes, touches my head, and I immediately choke with the tears that mount to my eyes. I can hardly hear the benedictions that he pronounces over me. His voice is already hoarse.

I fancy that I am already burning on the big twisted candle that mother has prepared. Sanctified, I leave the circle of its light—to me it is like white, warm hands shining behind the benedictions and tears—and stand under my mother's shaking hands.

When I am near her, I quiet down a little. I feel more at ease when I see her tears. I hear her simple, heartfelt prayers. I do not want at all to come out from under her hands. And actually I begin to feel cold as soon as the murmur of the benedictions ceases over my head.

Everyone is in haste to go to shul.

"Gut yom-tov!" Father quietly approaches mother and shakes hands with her.

"Gut yom-tov!" mother answers with lowered eyes.

I remain alone at home. The candles burn on, holy and warm. I take my place at the wall to say the Silent Prayer at once.

The benedictions that father has spoken over my head still sound in my ears. I beat my chest while reciting the confession of sins. I am afraid, for I probably have committed more sins than are enumerated in the prayer book.

My head grows hot. The letters of the sacred writing begin to spread in height and width. Jerusalem sways before my eyes. I should like to hold up the holy city with the thick prayer book that I clutch tightly with both hands.

Alone I cry to God and do not leave the wall until I can no longer think of anything to pray for.

The children now return from shul. The house is deserted, the table empty. Only the white tablecloth gleams dimly under the stumps of the half-burnt candles. They smoke. We do not know what to do with ourselves. So we go to sleep.

Next morning when I wake up, everyone has long since gone to shul. Again I am alone in the house. I remember everything that I am supposed to do. I only pour water over my fingers, I do not even brush my teeth, and with parched mouth I begin to pray. Gentile schoolmates come in; they want to do their homework with me. I do not move from the spot until I have finished praying.

I run to see my grandfather. He is old and sick and he too has remained alone at home. The Rabbi of Bobruisk (grandfather is a follower of his) has ordered grandfather not to fast. He must take a spoonful of milk every hour. So I go to my grandfather to give him his milk.

Grandfather is praying. He does not even glance at me and bursts into soft weeping. The spoon with the milk shakes in my hand, my fingers are splashed. Grandfather's tears drop into the spoon, mingle with the milk. He barely wets his pale lips and weeps more copiously under my tending. Heavy-hearted, I return home.

"Bashutke, come and have a bite!" Our Sasha begs me to come to the kitchen and eat a piece of cold chicken with her. "You must surely be starved!"

I am angry at myself because I am not yet fasting through the whole day. Every year I beg mother to permit me to fast. I cannot eat after witnessing grandfather's tears, and after seeing father come home with his pale, drawn face. He comes from shul to rest a little. With his white lips, his white kittel, and his white socks he looks—God forbid—as though he were not alive at all. I fancy that his soul has already become very pure and that it shines through his white garments. I begin to pray more fervently. I want to be at least in some small measure as pious as father.

Mother stays at the shul through the whole day. Before the Musaf I go to see her to ask how she is. The cantor can no longer be heard. The men's section is half empty. Some have gone home to rest, others sit on the benches, their eyes on their prayer books. Boys play in the shul courtyard; some have apples to eat, some have pieces of challa with honey. But the women's section is full of stifled weeping. In every corner a woman sighs and laments.

"Lord of the Universe, Lord of the Universe!" The chant resounds on all sides.

Mother is weeping quietly. She can scarcely any longer see the little letters of her prayer book through her clouded spectacles.

I stand at some distance and wait. Mother catches

her breath, raises her weeping face, and nods to me to tell me that she is feeling well, although she resumes her weeping at once. I come closer to her. I do not know what to do among all these weeping mothers. I look down into the men's section. The cantor's white kittel and white skullcap are still. I look among the rows of tall candles for our two. They are burning among all the other candles, burning high into the air at either side of the holy ark.

Suddenly a humming and a clamor rise over the shul. It becomes full of men. There is a bustle, the air grows hot. Men throng around the cantor. The heavy curtain of the holy ark is drawn aside. Now there is silence, the air has become motionless. Only the rustle of prayer shawls can be heard. The men hurry toward the holy ark. The shining scrolls of the Torah, like princesses awakened from sleep, are carried out from the ark. On their white and dark red velvet mantles great stars gleam—shields of David embroidered in silver and gold. The handles are mounted with silver, encrusted with mother-of-pearl, and crowns and little bells hang from them.

Light glows around the scrolls of the Torah. All the men in the shul are drawn toward them. The scrolls are surrounded, escorted. The men crowd after the scrolls of the Torah, trying at least to catch a glimpse of them, send a kiss to them from a distance. And they, the beautiful scrolls of the Torah, tower high above the heads of the worshipers, above all the out-stretched hands, and move slowly through the shul.

I can hardly keep myself behind the handrail of the women's section. I should like so much to jump down, to fall straight into the embrace of the holy Torahs, or at least move closer to them, to their quivering light, at least touch them, kiss their bright glory. But the scrolls are already being carried back, back to the holy ark. From both sides of it the tall candles twinkle at them. The velvet curtain is drawn, darkness comes to my eyes.

As though to drown the sadness, the men begin at once to pray aloud.

I remain standing at the window. I am attracted by the men's section, its clamorous air, filled with white talesim, like upraised wings surging through the shul, covering every dark spot. Only here and there a nose or an eye peeps out. The talis stripes sway like stairs above the covered heads.

One talis billows up, emits a groan, and smothers the sound within itself. The shul grows dark. I am seized by fear. The talesim bend, shake, move upward, turn to all sides. Talesim sigh, pray, moan. Suddenly my legs give way. Talesim quiver, drop to the ground like heavy sacks. Here and there a white woolen sock sticks out. Voices erupt as from underground. Talesim begin to roll, as on a ship that is sinking and going down amid the heaving waves.

I do not hear the cantor at all. Hoarse voices out-shout one another. They pray, they implore, asking that the ceiling open for them. Hands stretch upward. The cries set the lamps shaking. At any moment now the walls will crumble and let Elijah the Prophet fly in.

Grown-up men are crying like children. I cannot stand it any longer. I myself am crying more and more. I recover only when I perceive at last a living, weeping eye behind a crouching talis, when I hear trembling voices saying to one another: "Gut yom-tov! Gut yom-tov!"

I run home, for soon everyone will be back from shul, and I must set the table. "Sasha, hurry, hurry, prepare the samovar!" I cry to the maid.

I drag the tin box of pastry from the cupboard. I empty it all out on the table—cakes, cookies, ginger-bread, wafers, all sorts of buns. There is no room left even for a glass of tea.

Sasha lights the lamp and carries in the cheerfully humming samovar. Even the samovar seems glad that it has survived, that it has been remembered. Now the voices of my brothers can be heard. They rush in like hungry animals, one after the other.

Mother, looking worn, enters with a soft smile on her face and says to everyone: "Gut yom-tov!"

"Gut yom-tov!" says the cook. She runs in from the kitchen and smiles a pale smile.

We are waiting for father. As always, he is the last

to come from shul. In high spirits we fall upon the food. Glasses of tea are poured and drunk.

We have saved ourselves. We are no longer hungry. May God give his seal upon a good year for all of us. So be it, amen!

SUKKOT

The day after Yom Kippur we wait for a messenger from God. Surely he must come after our prayers and tears of yesterday!

And then a peasant with a cartful of branches of red fir drives into the courtyard. He overturns his cart. Prickly branches fall down, heaped one upon the other.

The courtyard turns into a forest. There is a smell of tar, of pine. The branches are fresh as just after a rain. Like huge birds at rest the branches lie, and a fragrance comes from them like a song.

If one crawls up on the mountain of branches, it utters a groan and bends underfoot. If one rolls on it, the mountain collapses entirely.

"Why are you trampling the branches?" My brothers come running with outcries. "Do you think it's hay? Don't you know it's for the sukkah?"

They pull the branches from under my feet. Each branch comes up heavily from the ground, shakes itself free with its spikes.

I help to carry the branches into the sukkah, which

is not yet ready. Only the walls, made of long boards, have been set up and nailed. The roof is open. The sky looks in. My brothers climb up the ladders, stand on chairs, and hand the branches to one another, shaking them as one shakes the Sukkot palm branch.

The branches open up like fans. Soon the sukkah is covered as a head is covered with a cap. It stands in the middle of the courtyard, alluring and beckoning, like a little house in the woods.

The branches are piled up on it so thickly that no little star from heaven will shine through the dark green. Inside the sukkah it is cool and dim. Only through the holes in the walls little patches of light creep through. And the points of light gleam and quiver, trying hard to slip in.

In the middle of the sukkah a long table and benches have been set up. There is no floor. Bare ground is underfoot. The legs of the table and of the benches rest in the damp earth, which sticks to one's feet.

We do not go out of the sukkah. We imagine that we are in a country house. We stretch out on the benches, pursue and intercept the patches of light that shine through the walls, and with our heads high in the air we gaze at the roof of branches as though it were a sky with stars. We shiver when a drop of dew falls on us.

We intone a song, by way of announcing to everyone that the sukkah is ready, that the holiday has come.

People look out of the windows of our apartment. "Look," they say, "the sukkah is ready!"

Suddenly someone calls out: "Children, the shames has brought the palm branch from the shul!"

We rush into the house. It too has become different. There is a smell of osier. Little leaves litter the

floor and their fragrance fills the whole apartment. And where is the palm branch?

There it stands by a corner window. It stands so wretchedly, leaning on the pane. Its head is bent to one side; perhaps it is trying to see through the glass whether a bit of the sky of its native land is shining there. Its long, narrow leaves are pressed together. I go to the palm branch. I am afraid to touch it. Its edges are sharp, like the edge of a sword.

"Let me shake the palm branch!" I beg my brothers.

"Before father?"

"I just want to see whether it is a live one."

The palm branch shakes in my hands; I shake with it. It makes a little wind around itself. I fancy that I am in the Land of Israel, under a shady palm tree.

How has the palm branch got here?

"Abrashke, what do you think?" I ask my brother insistently. "Has the palm branch come directly here from Palestine? What do you think it was there—a tree, or a branch broken off the tree? Who brought it here?"

"What is today—Passover, and you think you've got to ask questions?"

My brother does not know the answer himself, and he is trying to wriggle out of it.

"Listen," he says, "I think the palm branch has torn itself out of the earth. It wanted to have a look at what is going on in the world. So it ran away from home, and in one night"—he lowers his voice as though he himself were frightened—"in one night it grew up here, by our window."

I want to believe him, but I don't want him to be always right.

"But it's just been brought from the shul!" I remind him.

"And what would you say if you knew that the palm branch was wrapped in straw and packed in a big wooden chest? I've seen merchandise that is transported that way by train."

"Ah, do you think that the palm branch would travel like that with all the unclean goods? The rebbe would slap you if he could hear how you're talking about the palm branch. And look, why is it so fresh and green? It would have been smothered in a chest."

I touch the palm branch again. Its thin green leaves quiver like the long strings of a harp that is being tuned.

"Wait, palm branch," I comfort it while shaking it, "father will come soon, take you in his hands, offer a benediction over you—and then you won't feel so cold and strange in our house."

And where is the etrog?

The yellow citron, plump and big, is sprawled like a Pharaoh on a soft bed in the middle of the silver sugar box. In the place of the sugar, which has been removed, the citron gives off a fragrance like an emperor's. And where has it come from?

Now father is entering the house, my brothers after him.

"Come on, let us offer the benediction over the palm branch!"

Father looks at the palm branch, at the citron. He takes the citron out of its bed and puts it beside the palm branch. They nestle against each other. Are they perhaps natives of the same land?

And father, his eyes lowered, speaking the benediction aloud, as though taking an oath, pulls the palm branch upward, lowers it, places it near his heart, takes it away, shakes it to one side, to the other. The palm branch bends, sways. Its head trembles. Its long leaves stretch forward, all of themselves, into praying hands.

And the moment father stops, the palm branch composes its quivering body.

"Here, do you want to say the palm branch benediction?" Father hands it to the elder brother.

The palm branch passes from hand to hand. All the six brothers have fallen upon it; they shake it, break it, fence with it as with a sword. Barely surviving, it is put back near the window.

The finished sukkah stands waiting a whole day before at last they go to eat in it.

During the day it has absorbed the odor of pine, its

walls and the damp earth underfoot have dried. When evening comes, father and my brothers put on their coats as though preparing to go away. They go to eat supper in the sukkah.

Neither mother nor I nor the cook goes there. The three of us have only been allowed to go up to the door of the sukkah to hear father's benediction over the kiddush cup.

And the meals are served to those in the sukkah through a little window, as through a hole, one plate after another. My brothers can make believe that the plates with the food come to them straight from heaven.

Do they give a thought to us who have been left in the house?

In the apartment it is cold. It seems empty, and it feels as if there were no doors and windows. I sit with mother and eat without zest.

"Mother, why have we been left here with the servants, as though we too were servants? What kind of holiday is that, mother?" I keep tormenting her. "Why do they eat apart from us?"

"Ah, my little child, they're men," says mother, sadly, as she eats her piece of cold meat.

Suddenly the kitchen is in uproar. The maids run back and forth between the courtyard and the house.

"Mistress, it's beginning to rain!"

"Take the whole meal at once, so that they can say the blessings quickly!" Mother too is upset.

I am glad that it is raining in the middle of supper. For mother and me the holiday is so sad!

Suddenly—bang!—a thunderclap comes. I look through the window to see whether the sukkah has fallen apart. It is flooded with water.

In a trice the branches have been soaked through, turned flat and thin. Water drips on the table in the sukkah, it drips from the branches, from the walls. The maids run to and fro with covered plates in their hands. The rain is pattering on the plates, trying to uncover them.

Through the noise of the rain I hear father's benedictions. My brothers' high voices merge into the rain.

And one after the other, with their collars up, they run out of the sukkah. We look at them as though we had not seen them for a long time. They invade the apartment like people coming from another world.

Thus a few days go by. Now the sukkah is taken apart altogether. Board after board is pulled off. The walls are folded up. The roof of branches falls in, breaks up underfoot. The courtyard is filled with little needles.

The sukkah vanishes as if it had never been there.

The palm branch is taken down from the window ledge.

"Look what's become of it!" My brothers make fun of it. "It's like an old, old man, all dried up and toothless."

"Please," I beg of them, "weave some toy for me, a little basket or something like that!"

My brother Aaron sets to work. He has long, deft fingers. He tears one leaf after another from the palm branch. Each leaf whistles, bends. My brother's fingers dart about, splice it. He cuts narrow ribbons of it, plaits them into strips. One is fitted into another, and there it is, all ready, a little basket, a little trough, a table or a chair. Of the tall palm branch there remains only a hollow stalk.

And the etrog has been forgotten altogether. The cook has thrown it into a pan of boiling water, scalded it alive. The plump fruit has been boiled down to a saucer of thick juice.

There is a pull at my heart. The holiday has been boiled away. May Simchat Torah come soon, when the whole town, as it always seems, will be visiting us.

SIMCHAT TORAH

ONCE a year we children are allowed freely to make merry in the shul. From evening on we pant from the boisterousness of the hakkafot.

The shul is packed full of people. There is no place in which to get away from the boys. Even little girls come to the men's section for the hakkafot, and together with the boys they crowd around underfoot. The lamps seem to burn with a new flame. The holy ark is open, the scrolls of the Torah are carried out of it, one after the other. All of them are dressed up in little holiday mantles.

The shul is glorified like a holy temple. Men dance and stamp with the scrolls of the Torah in their hands. We children dance and stamp with them.

Like little wild creatures we run around the lectern, jumping up on it at one side, jumping down at the other. The wooden steps groan under our feet.

We push and chase one another; each of us wants to run around the lectern as many times as possible. We are not given time to touch or stroke its carved handrail, not even to catch our breath.

The rattles shake in our hands; the shul is filled with their noise. The paper flags whistle, flutter after us, and tear in the wind.

The shames hides in a corner. He fears that we will push the walls apart. Now it seems that the books on the stands are beginning to slip. He begs us: "Children, will there be no end of this? We've had enough! You'll upset the whole shul!"

We cannot stop. Our heads are whirling. We cannot stand on our feet.

I am exhausted when I drag myself home behind my brothers with my torn flag in my hand.

Next day, from early morning on, our apartment is in a bustle. Preparations are under way. Guests are expected.

We hurry to go to shul. We hurry to get through with the praying as soon as possible. Even before the end of the service, the men gather in clusters and ask each other in whispers: "Well, has it been decided to whom we are going first for the kiddush?"

"Sh-sh-sh! Sha! Uh! Ah!"

"Reb Shmul Noah has invited the whole shul!" someone whispers.

"Oh, then there'll be plenty to drink! Don't you think so, Reb Hershl?" This question is addressed to a thin man with a red nose.

"You're asking me? Well, then, let's first go to Reb Shmul Noah's. I'd say that he is a quite respectable householder!"

Then the whole shul pours out into the street.

"Why do you dawdle? Come on, faster, there are still plenty of places to go to!"

"Today the Jews will get drunk!" The gentile passers-by smile.

Even the fat monk standing in the road moves of his own accord to one side to let them pass. The whole congregation invades our apartment, it becomes crowded and hot.

"Gut yom-tov! Gut yom-tov! Gut yom-tov, baleboste!"

The women withdraw to one side. The crowd at once makes its way to the tables. "What is on the platters?" they ask one another.

The guests rub their hands with pleasure, push the chairs about, look at the table. Decked out as for a wedding, the table almost bends under the waiting feast. There are slices of cake, tarts, sponge cake with honey, platters of pickled herring, chopped liver, eggs in goose fat, calf's-foot jelly, fried udders. And bottles of wine and spirits stand on parade like soldiers.

"Why are you so mulish? Let another fellow have a chance too!" A tumult arises around the table.

"Why should you always be first? This is not the shul when people are called to the scroll of the Law!"

"He is more interested in drink than in anything else, so let him go through," the others laugh.

"Sha, here comes Reb Shmul Noah! To your

health, Reb Shmul Noah! To your health, raboisai!"

Father, as always, is the last to come from shul. In his long holiday coat, with his hat on his head, he looks taller, broader. "To your health, le-chayim, gut yom-tov!" he replies.

Father's high hat shakes on his head. He removes it and keeps his head covered with his skullcap. Then he asks: "Raboisai, have you made kiddush?"

"And you, our hosts?"

Several men stand up to make kiddush all at once: "Blessed be the Creator of the fruit of the vine—"

They begin to sway. The wine is sipped. They attack the brandy, they eat, they take morsels from each platter.

"Le-chayim, hostess! Your herring is a herring!"

"And the petcha a rare treat!"

Mother's face shines with pleasure.

Suddenly, like a jester at a wedding, the shames rises from the table. "Who wants to say mi-sheberach?" he asks. "Who will begin?"

A man with a long white beard rises from his seat, clears his throat, strokes his beard, moves sideways, parts his dense mustache, as though the beard and the mustache hindered him from opening his mouth.

"Mi-sheberach—" He begins in a singsong voice, swinging his body.

"Have you heard? How much does he give? How much has he pledged?"

The shames prances from one to another, and just

as if he were presenting a wedding gift to a bridal couple, he sings out loudly the name of the donor and the amount of the promised contribution.

"Why does he put cold towels on our heads? Where is some more drink? Hand us that bottle! Why do you keep it up there?"

Empty bottles roll away. New ones are opened, as though the party were only beginning. Glasses and goblets are filled, wine splashes on the tablecloth. Suddenly the man with the white beard bangs the table and cries out: "Silence!"

He closes his eyes and utters a sigh so deep that it sounds as though he were tearing out a piece of his heart and casting it far from him. His sigh runs over the table like a tremor. And suddenly—as if coming from afar, growing out of the sigh—there begins, in a low tone, the Rabbi's Song.

There is a humming. The old man's head is swaying. His brow is knitted. His lips and mustache are aquiver. Gradually he bewitches everyone. Pale faces begin to blaze. Eyes close. And in one breath all of them chant the song—voice after voice, higher and higher.

The melody spreads, swells, flares like a fire. The people swim in the song. With closed eyes they sway, bang the table; they seem to be trying to make the table itself sing, to wrench themselves free of the earth.

Some cry with fear, others sink into lamentation,

still others pray or weep. The melody is full of tears that do not fall. Some of the guests snap their fingers. Hands are outstretched. One man seizes his beard in his hand and supports it firmly—perhaps thus to hold his leaping heart.

Suddenly the lamentation stops. Joy breaks out.

"Ah, fellow Jews, there is a God in the world!" The white-bearded guest cranes his neck, as though the All-Highest himself were shedding glory upon him from above.

"Why are you sitting, friends? Today is Simchat Torah, the festival of the Torah—the rabbi said that one must make merry, dance!"

A hand and a foot shoot out, as if tearing loose from the body, and let themselves go.

The table is pushed to one side, the chairs are kicked away. The walls themselves seem to be swaying. The tablecloth slips. Pieces of cake and some glasses fall to the floor. The men begin to leap, to stamp in one spot. They turn the flaps of their coats, and they form little dance circles. Their shoulders are bent, their hands are interlocked, almost as if tied together. Shoulder to shoulder, each hangs on the other. They do not let go, as though they feared that if they were left alone they would fall in pieces.

People cannot see one another, no one sees himself. The dancers' boots kick high curves. Sometimes their feet give out.

A fresh back straightens itself and with a fresh

strength the newcomer hurls himself into the seething dance as into a fire. The whole ring of dancers drags after him. Now no one remains sitting at the table. The table itself takes motion and pushes toward the revelers.

"Reb Shmul Noah, our host, what are you waiting for? Get up!"

And father, always so quiet, so calm, moves from his place, makes his way toward the dancing men, and falls into the whirling ring. The chain of people gives a tug and swallows him.

From my corner I watch father. I look for him among the dancers. There is his head, slightly bent to one side, his eyes lowered, his long beard afloat. There he is, whirling as in a sweet dream, his whole body melting with pleasure.

My father is dancing! I can no longer keep still. "Mother, may I?"

The women in the corners are thrilled. Once a year their husbands make merry.

"Mother, please let me! I too want to dance, to have a whirl with father!" I pull my mother's sleeve.

"What are you saying, my child, you'll be trampled down on the spot! You see!"

With a shout, a tall, thin Jew bounces into the room. He turns a somersault and lands on his feet. He twists on the floor like a worm, and in one jump lands in the kitchen. "Make way, make way!" he cries.

"Oi, woe is me!" The cook is frightened. "Reb Laizer, have pity on me! What do you want to do in the kitchen?"

She has recognized in him a neighbor from our courtyard. But the thin newcomer does not listen—she might as well not have spoken. He snatches up the big fork and drags out of the oven a large earthenware pot full of the black, sticky delicacy called kulaie. The pot turns over, its contents spill out over the visitor. He turns black like a Negro, runs back into the room, and further excites the drunken dancers.

All of them are dizzy; they can barely stand on their feet. They drop into the chairs exhausted. With their heads bent, they lie for a while as in a faint.

"Raboisai, gentlemen, we have still to visit Reb Mendel!" One of them comes to with a shout.

All of them jump up from their seats as though they had been lashed, and run with tottering legs out into the street. Father runs with them.

When the first stars come out, father appears in the doorway, a little drunk, staggering. He is ashamed to enter the apartment. Like a sheaf of grain falling he tumbles onto his bed.

We are ashamed with him.

THE FIRST SNOW

AFTER the Fearful Days come dragging, humdrum days, days without meaning, without savor—short, gray days.

Outside it rains constantly; the rain, it seems, has forgotten to stop. The windowpanes are lashed and spattered, the glistening raindrops roll down on them in little tears, as though they were weeping.

At home it is dark even during the day.

The day has no sooner begun than it flickers out. Even the wall clock ticks quietly, slowly, draws out the hours and chimes them hoarsely. I do not know where to escape from sadness. There is something like a choked weeping in the patter of rain.

"Havah," I say to the cook again and again, "someone is scratching at the door. Open it!"

"Oi, let me alone! I wish someone would come! But who would come when it is pouring without end?"

"Don't you hear? Someone is splashing in the mud!"

"Small wonder! It's been raining and blowing for a whole day and night!"

"No, there are many feet stamping in the courtyard!"

"Well, look at her! There's no way of getting rid of the girl! Now you'll see, little goose, there's no one there. What's that?"

Havah stops, her mouth wide open. From the dim hall a pair of dark eyes glitter like a wolf's from behind a tree. Two tangled beards poke in at the door. They are dripping with rain.

"Robbers!" I pull Havah by the sleeve.

"What on earth is this?" Havah, frightened too, is infuriated.

"Cabbage, little lady, we've brought fresh cabbage!" The beards shake and a heavy breath wafts toward us. Two tall peasants, drenched through and through, drag in heavy, wet sacks behind them. They are both dripping like thatched roofs. Their boots squeak with water.

[116]

They stop in the hallway. They scratch their heads and stand for a while, as if lost. They are feeling dry ground underfoot.

"Why do you stand there, you soul of a dog? Don't you see the door?" They push one another and stamp their feet.

"Fie on your head!" The other one spits. The sacks are heavy—they might be filled with stones. The peasants are panting. Their breath is like a mist; the hall seems full of vapor.

"Here, go slow! Ah, what mud, what dirt!" The cook berates them. "You've messed up everything, like pigs. Don't walk another step with your muddy boots! There, there, in the corner!" Havah has taken up her post in the middle of the kitchen, and does not permit the peasants to make one needless move. "What a time you've chosen! Couldn't you come on a dry day? You've brought all the mud in the village here. I've just scrubbed the kitchen. And how is the cabbage? Probably rotten through and through!"

From the sacks white, round heads of cabbage fall out, so curled, so clean—each little head seems decked with a white lace coverlet. Not even stained by the muddy sacks! Little head after little head, one tumbles out after the other. Each rolls out bottom up; they rub cheeks, huddle against one another.

A huge mountain of cabbages has piled up. There is a whiff of fresh, strong odor, as though suddenly a whole field of cabbage had been planted in the middle of the kitchen. The kitchen has come back to life and we with it. Havah at once sets to work. She rolls up her sleeves, brings in tubs and pails.

"Children, do not climb on the cabbage!" she says in a commanding tone. "Sasha, bring the table from the cellar, wash it clean."

A narrow, long table with an iron cleaver in the center of it has been pushed up to the cabbage pile. I feel a heart stab, as if the hangman in person had taken up his post in the kitchen.

A head of cabbage is thrown on the table. It slides under the teeth of the cleaver, and in a flash it is cut into shreds. Another head is pushed up to the cleaver, which moves up and down. Shreds of cabbage fly like feathers and fall into the tubs placed underneath.

On the sliced cabbage water is poured; grains of pepper are thrown into it. The water gushes, mounts to the surface, seethes into the cabbage that keeps dropping down from the table into the tubs.

The pails, the barrels are full. Disks of red carrot dot the pallor of the cabbage. It is weighted down with a big stone placed on it as a lid; the cabbage cannot escape from under it.

I accompany the tubs to the dark cellar. There in the damp air the once living white, hard cabbage will quickly soak through and ferment. We children fall upon the leftover sweet little hearts and scoop them out with our teeth.

Nor do we miss the day when cucumbers are pickled.

"Havah, give us a cucumber, we'll help you clean it!"

"So you've already got wind of the cucumbers too? I know your tricks!"

The cook admonishes us not to pass over any cucumber with a black speck on it. We rub the cucumbers, polish them like shoes, till their green skins shine.

It is almost unbearable to see the polished cucumbers laid out in a trough and buried under the yellow flowerets of dill and other sharp and bitter herbs. The cucumbers are soaking in a damp little grave.

Each of us chooses a particularly shining cucumber, snatches it from the trough, and cracks it like a nut between his teeth.

"You brats!" cries the cook. "What have I been telling you? You'll eat up all the cucumbers!"

And we, with our mouths full, shout at her: "Ugh, you witch! You want to soak everything, get everything moldy with your sour pickle! Who will be able even to recall the taste of a fresh green cucumber?"

And with a sour taste on our tongues we take ourselves out of the kitchen. Rain is pouring down. We feel moldy ourselves.

Suddenly one morning, when I wake up, there is a miracle. Light shines in my eyes! The rain has stopped, the whole apartment is bright! The windows are clear, the panes are dry, and through them come white shafts of light.

"Snow! Snow has fallen!" We cannot tear ourselves from the windows.

The courtyard does not look like our courtyard. Yesterday it was gray and gloomy, and now it stands there all dressed in white. Snow is falling on it from above like a shimmering veil. It must have been snowing all night long.

The roofs and the balconies already lie under high, puffed-up featherbeds of snow. There are piles of snow at the doors. The stairs are covered with a thick white carpet. And it is still falling from the sky, the white, silvery snow; the air is glittering with snowflakes, as though the sky in the middle of the day were scattering its stars on the earth. Our eyes are washed clear by the first snow. Or perhaps I have been given a pair of new, white eyes?

The little birds have suddenly flown away. And from the trees little nestling clumps of snow peep out, like frozen straylings.

"Let's see who'll be first to step on the snow!" Abrashke presses his face to the windowpane; his flattened nose sticks to the glass. "Look, snow has fallen between the windowpanes too!"

Long, narrow pads of white cotton have been unrolled between the double windows; they glitter like real snow with the silver threads that are laced over them. And from the cotton there protrude shamefacedly a few red and pink paper flowers that are wondering how they have grown here.

My brother breathes on the glass, passes his finger over it, and draws a terrifying head with hair. We burst into laughter. The little flowers begin to quiver. Abrashke, the prankster, is pleased when he frightens anyone, even if it is only a paper flower.

"Get away from the windows, you rascals! That's all we need—someone to break a pane in this cold!"

We are driven away from the window. And we fancy that the white snow is falling behind us on our backs.

THE HANUKKAH LAMP

"CHILDREN, where are you all? Mendl, Avreml, Bashke, where have you all got lost?" Mother's high voice is heard from the shop. "Where do you run about for whole days? Come, father is waiting with the Hanukkah lights."

Where would we be? We are standing and warming ourselves at the stove. The day has almost gone. It is now dark. So we are waiting for the shop to be closed.

Mother runs out of the shop like a culprit, apologizes to herself: "Today is a sort of holiday, and I'm still tangled up in the shop. Let us at least gather the children and bless the Hanukkah lights."

All together we go to the big room, where father is waiting for us.

The room, although large, has only one small window. Father stands with his back to the window, and the scant light from outside is quite shut out. So all of us are standing in darkness, waiting for the little taper to be lighted.

Father's head is bent over the Hanukkah lamp. On the dark wall father's shadow bends too; it might be another father roaming about and looking for something on the wall. When his head turns to one side, the dark silver of the Hanukkah lamp glimmers. Like a sleepy moon it reveals itself, shining out from the corner where it was concealed, hidden from everyone.

The Hanukkah lamp is small, almost like a toy. But how many things are carved on its tiny silver wall!

In the center are two lions with fiery heads, open mouths; with their legs upraised they hold up the outspread tables of the Law. The tablets are blank, without a single letter on them, but they give forth a light as though they were packed full of sacred wisdom inside.

Around the lions there is a garden. It blooms, a real paradise—it has little vines with grapes, and familiar fruit fallen from the trees. A pair of birds peep out from the branches. And even a big serpent crawls there.

At either side of the paradise there stand on watch two silver pitchers, tiny too, but with fat, stuffed little bellies. They see to it that the paradise does not lack oil. And to gladden one's eyes there is under the lions and birds a little bridge, divided into eight little goblets that are waiting for a flame to go up from them. Father's white hands move among the goblets. From one—father begins with the first—he pulls out a tiny wick; then he tips a pitcher and pours a drop of oil into the goblet. The wick drinks in the oil, becomes soft and white, almost like a candle.

Father says a benediction and lights the wick. Only one light. Father does not even touch the other goblets. All seven of them stand as though superfluous, empty and cold.

It is not festive at all with only one light burning. My heart tightens, as though—God forbid—a memorial candle were burning.

Its flame is so little that it could be put out with one whiff. No reflection falls from the light onto the dark floor. Even the wall of the paradise is not much illumined. Of the two lions, only one receives a little warmth from below, the other does not even know that something is burning beside him.

My parents and my brothers have gone. I approach the light; I try to pull up its wick, hoping to brighten its flame. But there is nothing that I can grasp with my hand. I singe my fingers. The little flame burns, faints, flickers, trembles all the time. At any moment it will go out; it makes an effort to rise upward at least once, to lick a grape on the silver wall, or to warm one foot of the carved lion.

Suddenly, one after another, drops of thick oil begin to fall from the taper; they clog the little opening of the goblet, and they smother the little flame. The wick begins to smoke and smears the woodwork of the window.

A fresh gray stain is added to the stains that have remained on the window frame since last year's Hanukkah. All the stains shine above the solitary light, almost outshine the light itself. And when the big chandelier is lighted, the large flame of the lamp blows away the last breath of the Hanukkah light.

Why are mother's Sabbath candles tall and large? And why does big father bless such a tiny Hanukkah light?

THE FIFTH LIGHT

ONE light after another is kindled. Now all of five lights are burning in the Hanukkah lamp. All five have been lighted at one time. One candle fans the next and the flame of all five spreads from right to left over the Hanukkah lamp and now warms the whole silver paradise. Around the dining table, all the children, big and small, have gathered. The chandelier glows with a full holiday flame. From the kitchen comes one fragrant odor after another.

The boiled salmon cools off there under a little pond of sauce. Onion ringlets that have been cooked with the salmon are caught in the sauce as though frozen in ice.

The grieven have already turned black and hard, although their little ears are drowned in fat. A pot of fat sizzles on the hot coals. The kitchen is hot. Havah's cheeks are aflame. She stands before the open oven and with iron tongs in her hands she reaches for the pans. Now she heats one, now she smears another with a piece of greased paper; she pours out a spoon-

ful of liquid dough, or removes a freshly fried latke
from the pan. Hot, plump, they glisten, the latkes,
with pearls of fat, and they jump on the fire like new-

born little babies when they are slapped with the hand.

We watch the cook as though she were a magician.

"Havah, the thick latke is for me, isn't it?" Abrashke sticks out his stuffed cheeks, which seem about to burst.

"You'll end up by getting a tummy-ache! How many latkes must you stuff yourself with? This brat doesn't give me a minute of respite!" Havah grumbles while she goes on frying, and piles up platters of hot, fresh latkes.

We laugh in delight and lick our fingers. The latkes are sliding in fat. We crunch the grieven. What shall we get at first?

And there, suddenly, is a pile of little pieces of wood on the table—tiny blocks, shaped like little kegs, poured out of a box. A lotto game!

Hard white cards are dealt out to us. On the cards, from top to bottom, there are black numbers, all in a hodgepodge. A figure two stands beside a nine, a seven beside a three—a mixed-up kind of order. The game comes to an end when anyone is lucky enough to have covered all his numbers with the little wooden kegs, on which the same numbers are painted. The whole game is a matter of chance. Each time a block is drawn, everyone starts, as though the number had jolted his luck: "Eleven! Four! Seven!"

"The four is out! Here is the four!"

"Who has seven? No one has seven?"

The little block turns in my brother's hand, is pushed upon the table.

Number seven rolls under the gleaming lamp like a black devil on one leg. The block merges with the number; the figures make my eyes dizzy.

"You clumsy fool! You've got a seven! Why don't you say so? Must you always have everything put under your nose?" Abrashke squeals behind my back.

"Will I win?"

"You blockhead! Do you think one wins so fast?"

Everyone puts in a word.

"What can you do with her? She is dreaming, she is asleep!"

"She has just eaten too many latkes! Can't you tell by her eyes?"

"What else? Don't talk such nonsense! Say rather that she doesn't even know how to write a seven!"

"Really?"

At this point I cannot stand it any longer. "The teacher says I'm a better pupil than you!" I answer them. "I know a seven very well—it's a lucky number!"

"You've almost missed your luck by sleeping!"

Out of fright, I no longer let the block go out of my sight. Suddenly I jump up. "Look!" I cry. "I've won, won, I've won in spite of you!"

Everyone turns to me, and together with all of them I gaze at my card, miraculously all covered with the blocks.

"A fool always has luck!" Abrashke shoots out.

Everyone envies me. Even the kindly Mendl bangs the table with his cards, as though rapping my hands.

"I lacked one number, one single number, to win!" He frets and fumes.

"Never mind, you'll win some other time! To her the few kopeks she has won mean a great deal," Abrashke says, leering in my direction.

My joy is ruined. The money burns my fingers.

"Better see how the teetotum will spin!" Abrashke twirls the leaden top on the table.

The single leg of the top has barely touched the slippery oilcloth and it is spinning as fast as anything. It zooms, whistles like a wind, as if it were spinning up into the air.

Everyone's eyes are fixed on the teetotum. As it spins, its sides look sunken in. The letters gimel and nun have flashed out once and evaporated. But as though the top were losing its breath, the little wind begins to subside, the leg spins more and more slowly.

The leaden sides with the carved letters on them become plain. The gimel, the shin, the heh, and the nun are nodding to us with their little heads, as though they had come from afar.

"I'll bet you anything you like that it will stop on the gimel."

"How could it do otherwise, if that's what you want!"

Each of us stares at the gimel, trying to intercept it with his eyes, stop it in its path. And now it seems that the teetotum is about to stop, on the gimel, which stands for "good." The shin, which stands for "bad," and comes right after, trips the gimel, as it were. The gimel falls on its face, and the shin stands up in the middle of the table.

"Now will you bet again?"

"Well, what is there to talk about? It's a holiday today! Let's play a game of cards, eh?"

With new ardor we fall upon the cards. And the cards themselves strike our eyes with their painted faces.

Only a queen has a white, smooth face, a slender figure. A king occupies the whole card with his body, trying to give it more weight with his fatness.

The knaves, who are younger, want to show off with their skillfully twisted mustaches. Sometimes the two knaves on one card appear to be pushing each other with their sawed-off legs. Each would like to be in the middle.

[131]

It is a science in itself to know the value of each card.

"We're playing Twenty-One, eh?"

My brothers grow excited. Again and again one of them shuffles the cards, thumbs them with a gesture of airing them. He blows, spits on his fingers, pushes the cards out of one hand into the other. Suddenly he cries out: "Cut!"

Another player picks up a portion of the cards and places them on the remaining ones.

"Tap on them!" the first commands.

"Why do you give orders all the time?" cries another. "That's enough shuffling of the cards! What do you want to make of them—new cards? Do you think you're frying latkes?"

"One, two—here's a card. And here is one for you. One, two, three—"

The cards are lined up like men on a battlefield. With bated breath all of us watch them slipping out from under my brother's thumb. We sit as on needles. We are afraid to see what card has turned up.

"My partner surely has a better hand," each of us thinks to himself, and jams his cards more tightly into his fist, until he crumples them altogether, as though his winning chances depended only upon hiding his hand from his partner's sight. And he has to guard his secret!

The hardest thing to do is to let the cards lie on the table and not look at them, but keep them in mind.

So the cards are arrayed in rows face down on the table, and each of us sits and waits for a miracle: perhaps he will be the winner. If it turns out that he is holding a knave, his heart sinks: it's all over—not he but his partner will win!

"Don't be so conceited!" one begins to tease the other. "Sometimes a low card is better than the big king."

"What have you got against kings?"

"Do you imagine that by not saying anything you've made your cards silent?"

"I don't need your kings—I've got a card that's better than a queen!"

"Let's see, let's see!" All of us fall upon the boaster, Abrashke.

"How can you believe him, the thief!" cries the other. "And why do you kick all our chairs? Look, you've made me drop a card out of my hand!"

"I've made you do it?" Abrashke apes him. "You fool, what are you babbling? You're dropping them from fright!"

"You chump, give me back my card, or you'll be out of the game!"

"Is that so? Just wait!" Abrashke rolls on the floor. "Now I've got you all in my left whiskers! Here she lies, the queen, her face up!"

Abrashke whinnies in his glee at having been the first to see another's precious card.

"Give it to me, it's my card!" the other protests. "One doesn't play with such thievish tricks! Such a game doesn't count!"

"And how do you know what is allowed and what isn't? A new sage!"

"What a rascal! He turns the world upside down!"

My brothers fall upon one another, a tumult arises around the table. The cards are pushed about, the chairs move here and there. One elbows in, another starts a fight. One slaps the other in the face and is slapped in turn. A real war has broken out—they might almost be shooting with guns.

"Anyhow, it's not your queen!" the victim persists.

"Why?" Abrashke refuses to give in. "On the floor or on the table, it's a card, not a fig!"

"Take that, you dog! This time all your tricks won't help!"

"Hush, children, how long will you keep up this noise? It's not possible to go to sleep! It's already midnight!"

My brothers stop, exchange glances. Father's voice from the bedroom is like a dash of cold water on all of us.

I quietly gather up the cards. My head seems to be swelling—all the cards are fighting in my head.

The kopeks I have won keep me from falling asleep. They lie under my pillow, but it is as though they were crawling out from under the feathers, mur-

muring, pricking my ears. I am afraid to touch them—
they might as well be stolen money.

I can hardly wait for the morning, and I give them
to the first beggar who knocks at our door.

HANUKKAH MONEY

Mother once told me that I was born during Hanukkah, on the day of the fifth light. But who knows that in our house? None of my brothers ever thinks about when he came into the world.

"All right, you were born—an event indeed! What of it?" My brothers laugh. "What do you want, to be born all over again?"

And my father booms out: "What's this? A new holiday, all of a sudden? Only a goyish head could have thought that up!"

So all I had to rejoice about at Hanukkah were the two ten-kopek pieces of Hanukkah money that we younger children received from father and grandfather.

For the money we would hire a sleigh and take a ride. To go riding with a real horse was a treat we were ready for on any day. The two silver ten-kopek pieces sang and rang in our ears like the bells of the sleigh that would take us all over the town. Grandfather's coin was particularly shining, as though he had had it scrubbed for us in honor of Hanukkah.

On the day of Hanukkah, early in the morning,

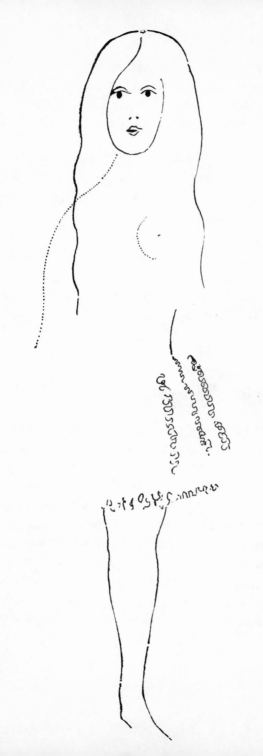

Abrashke and I run to grandfather's house. If the old man is still asleep, we'll wake him up. Perhaps he has completely forgotten that there is Hanukkah in the world?

Grandfather lives (how did that ever happen to him?) in a goyish street. Its name is Officers' Drive. Probably he lives there because it is near the great square of the synagogues.

It is a street of little white houses—the whole street is white. It is the quietest street in the city—no shops, no din. There one can really fall asleep. One cannot even laugh out loud in the middle of the street. Immediately, from behind the flowerpots that block up the windows, the flowered caps of old ladies stick out; and they shake their heads and call out: "Stop laughing, you brats!"

As though a sick grandfather were lying in every little house!

And the houses are so low that perhaps all that one can do is to lie down in them. And what if a tall man should want to stand up? He would have to bend over double. Probably that is why my grandfather and grandmother grow shorter every year.

Some of the little houses are quite sunken in. It seems as though the aged people who live in them are growing into the earth, and one wonders whether the flowerpots are standing on the window sills or growing from the street.

From inside one neither sees nor hears anything.

The little houses are wrapped in snow as in thick, warm blankets. Their walls are stopped up, like deaf ears. The wind blows the snow onto the windows, it fills up the cracks, but the old lace curtains do not shake even the tiniest bit. Over the roofs, the chimney smoke roams freely, like a drunken goy. It seems as if it felt too hot from the heat in the houses: the smoke is restless, stretches to all sides, tries to get out of the chimneys by force. The little houses sweat under snow, a white sweat.

"Here, here, you dreaming slowpoke! Why are you gaping in all directions?" Abrashke suddenly bursts out into resounding laughter and pelts me with snowballs from across the street. "You crazy duck, stop yelling! People will be coming from all doors!"

"In this cold? What do you want to bet?"

From behind a fence a white tree looms up—apparently an old tree. The snow is piled up on it like a dozen cushions on grandmother's bed. The branches can hardly bear up under it. Abrashke scrambles up the fence, climbs the tree, and gives it a shake.

The whole tree begins to quiver. Lumps of snow fall from it like stones. A bare branch cracks and breaks.

"You wicked creature!" I protest. "Isn't there enough snow on the street for you? Does it bother you if it lies on the tree?"

"It's my tree just as much as yours! Are you a close relative of it, or what?"

I feel like running into a little house, no matter whose. Perhaps a little old woman will be standing behind the door, and I can hide from Abrashke in her warm, wadded skirts.

Grandfather's house is at the very end of the street. It is a little house like all the others—the same flower-pots, the same carved shutters with panels cut like candy bars and with snow stuffed into their little holes; there is the same smoke over the roof. But the house looks whiter and warmer than all the others.

Abrashke runs up to the door and instantly pulls the bell cord. The bell gives a hoarse cough and falls silent.

"Ah, so you're here already, children! I'm only about to go to market, and they're already coming for Hanukkah money!"

This welcome is from Fride, grandmother's old cook. She opens the door. A shawl is around her shoulders. "B-r-r-r! What cold you have brought with you! Come in, quickly. Is it really so cold in the street? Shall I put another kerchief around me, like you, Bashinke?"

She stamps her feet, and as she stamps her summer freckles jump on her face. In the winter they look like dried drops of fat that she has forgotten to wash off. She is always in a hurry, she is always in a dither. She says that she is about to go to market. But she has already cooked her dinner. We can smell something roasting in the kitchen.

"Fride, will you let us taste a roasted potato?"

"How do you know that I'm roasting potatoes?"

"Fride, is grandfather still asleep?"

"Who is asleep? What's this talking of sleep? Isn't he studying the Talmud all the time? Scat!" She pushes the cat out of her marketing basket. "She's invented something new! Creeping into my basket!"

The noise awakens the cat. A gleam shoots from the slits of her eyes; she sees the snow sticking to our feet, lifts her tail, pricks up her whiskers, and stretches toward us to lick the flakes of cold snow. The snow melts under her nose and she begins to sneeze.

"A cat's brain!" Abrashke says, pulling her by the tail. "It would be better to go tell grandmother that we're here."

"Why bother the cat? She is such a lazybones! I can go much faster than she!"

Grandmother comes in. She moves silently, as though her gentle smile softened her footsteps too.

"Such cold, children, and yet you're here? You're surely on an important errand," she says smiling. "And take your things off quickly, Bashinke! Warm yourself by the stove—but look out, don't burn yourself. I've just closed the chimney."

Grandmother stands near us in bewilderment. "Do you want a glass of warm milk?" she asks. "It's so early, what shall I give you for a treat?"

She does not know what to do first—whether to help us to take our coats off or to go and look for a treat for us. Her white face and her white hair shine. The flowers on her cap are abloom as if it were mid-summer. She herself is soft, stout, warm like the heated white-tiled stove.

In this house there is no room to move around. Everywhere it is cluttered up with furniture and hangings, as though grandmother, in her constant fear of catching cold, were as much afraid of any bit of free space as of a draft.

"Grandmother, it's a holiday today, Hanukkah!" Abrashke assails her at once.

"What are you talking about? But even if it is Hanukkah, you shouldn't knock your grandmother down! May you be spared by the evil eye, you have grown recently!" And grandmother rocks on her short legs.

Abrashke is frightened. What bad luck, if grandmother should be angry!

"All the same, you're a good boy, Avreml!" Grandmother smiles. "Coming so early in the morning with the tidings! I was just going to ask grandfather. Without you I'd never have known, you little rascal! Well, first of all, go and kiss the mezuzah. Haven't your teachers told you to do that?"

"Grandmother, and what about me?" I put in. "I want to kiss it too!"

"Where are you pushing to, small fry? You're a girl, aren't you?" Abrashke shoves me away along with the cat, which is tangled up with my legs.

He is lucky. He is a boy, and he can show off. Perhaps it would really be better to be a cat instead of a short little girl whom he is always mocking.

"Stop teasing the little one!" Suddenly grandmother puts her hands to her head as though recalling something. "You haven't caught cold, God forbid? Come, I'll give you something, Bashinke!"

"Raspberries, grandma?" I run after her. I know that when grandmother says "a cold" she will hunt up a jar of raspberries that is stored away in her wardrobe with all the other jams.

"Here, Bashinke, take it with you," she says. "And tell mother to give you a glass of hot tea with raspberries before you go to sleep. Tell her it's a remedy for everything and the best cure for a cold."

"Grandma, where is grandpa?" my brother asks. "We don't see him."

"Go in—there he is, standing by the stove."

Through the half-open door of the dining room we see, shining like a white mirror, a great white-tiled stove, and next to the stove, swaying like a black shadow, our grandfather. And we thought that he was still asleep! Asleep, indeed! It seems to me that ever since we last saw him—it was on the Sabbath—he has been standing just that way next to the stove and has not even once lain down to sleep. He is wearing the same coat, a long one, of thin black lustrous material, and full of wrinkles like his forehead. The same coat, summer and winter—and under the coat his slight body vanishes, as though he had no body at all.

His face is shining. His eyes are pensive. With one hand he is stroking a small hair in his beard, with the other he seems to be unraveling a knot in the air, and he sways. It looks as if he were interpreting something for himself from a book that is lying on the table, and moving the debated text from one side of his head to the other.

He does not see the two of us. His spectacles have climbed up on his forehead, and his thick, bristling eyebrows conceal his eyes. His white beard falls like a pile of snow. And the patches of cheek that show from under his forelocks are also white. Single veins stand out red under his delicate skin, perhaps because they have been warmed up by the stove.

We are afraid to go close to him. His shadow sways against the white tiles. I fancy that grandfather is standing far from us, with one foot in the other world.

"Bashke, look!" My brother pulls my sleeve. "Look, the ten-kopek piece is lying on the table!"

Dear grandfather! He has thought even of that! And I imagined that he thought only of the things of God!

But grandfather still does not turn his head away from the window. The sun is shining and is reflected in his eyes, as though they had drawn in all the light of heaven. Now they seem to flash. In the window hangs the Hanukkah lamp of old, tarnished silver, with empty branches instead of candles. But grandfather's eyes, like a lighted taper, kindle all the eight branches at once.

"Grandpa!" We cannot wait while he seems so unaware of us—and then we stop, frightened by the sound of our own voices.

"Ha? What is it?" Grandfather wakes up suddenly as if from sleep. "Aige, I think someone has come in. Please go and see."

"It's just Alta's children, Avreml and little Bashke!" grandmother calls to him from her room.

Grandfather turns his white head toward us. Seeing us he smiles. His face crinkles up, and with this smile grandfather has changed, has become another man. His face has melted like warm wax.

"And I thought"—grandfather lets his glasses drop from his forehead and gazes at my brother from behind them—"I thought that Avreml is going to be bar-mizvah next year, God willing, and that he no longer thinks of Hanukkah money. Isn't that so, Avreml?" And grandfather lightly pinches his cheek.

"Well, come over here," he goes on, "shall I test you? Tell me"—his soft voice breaks—"how far have you got in the chumash? You've been studying with the rebbe for several seasons."

The ten-kopek coin gleams on the table. Abrashke's head turns. The silver piece tantalizes his eyes. It lies so near, quite near to him. He can almost touch it,

[145]

stroke it with his hand. He is dying to see what is stamped on the other side of it—will it be the same eagle as always, or not?

Grandfather's voice hums in Abrashke's ears, but Abrashke's hand itches to spin the coin over the table at least once. The oilcloth is slippery, and the coin would fly like a top. It might even slide off the table, and then it would be gone. Then he would have to look for it in all the cracks of the floor!

In his fright, Abrashke's round eyes pop out of his head. He says to himself that he must snatch the ten-kopek piece before grandfather starts questioning him and testing him about all the passages that he has learned and already forgotten.

And what if grandfather should think of taking the chumash out of the bookcase, and—of all things— should ask Abrashke to recite just as he has to do it in cheder with the rebbe? That way the whole day will go by! And it will get dark! And where will he get a driver and sleigh, where a horse? Who will wait for him? All the boys are already out riding, packed into the sleighs, and he—

Abrashke feels his heart sinking. He will fall asleep here, he thinks, together with grandfather, near the warm stove.

Abrashke thrashes about, hot and restless, as though he instead of the firewood were burning inside the hot stove. It is heartbreaking to see him. His fingers tremble. His head seems swollen. And his eyes sparkle, as though the silver ten-kopek piece had got into them.

"Ten kopeks!" Abrashke keeps saying to himself. And if he should get another ten kopeks from father, he would be able to ride all over town! What sleigh driver would not take him? He, Abrashke, needs only the silver coin in his hand. If he shows just one edge of it to Ivan the coachman, the man's eyes will pop out of his head. He will get excited, the knave—he will try to persuade Abrashke that nothing can equal his horse, his sleigh. Hasn't he inherited them from a rich landowner?

"In this sleigh of mine," Ivan will say, "there lies a black fur robe. Never mind if it looks like an old dead goat. The landowner's children used to cover themselves with the fur!"

And as for his horse—Ivan will even whistle with enthusiasm—all one needs to do is to whip it well, and it will fly like an eagle! It's no ordinary horse—the landowner's wife herself used to ride it.

"And what about my bells? Don't they ring like all the church bells at once? Just sit down, and let my horse get started—" Ivan's thick voice trumpets in my brother's ears.

Abrashke cannot stand it any longer. He lunges forward, seizes the coin.

"Eh, don't grab! Take your time. Why are you in such a hurry? You should be anxious to learn your bar-mizvah speech!"

Abrashke raises his head. Who is speaking? Not Ivan! Grandfather's bony hand is resting on his tense fingers.

"Baruch, give them their ten kopeks. It's a bit of joy for the children! Don't you see," grandmother says to grandfather, "his skin is burning! The boy cannot sit still. And the little one is standing there almost in a daze!"

Holding our breath, we run out of grandfather's warm little house, clutching the ten-kopek piece.

My brother tears through the streets. The snow is actually burning under his feet. He does not stop twisting his hand; he seems to be trying to make the silver coin tinkle in his glove.

One thought is drumming in his head: "Is there still a sleigh to be had? A horse?"

I stop for a moment—one of my galoshes has slipped off.

"That's what happens to you when you start something with a girl! You're just a fool!" Abrashke yells at me instead of helping me. "Will you stop dawdling? First grandpa, and now you, with your galoshes! All the sleighs will be taken!"

"It isn't my fault! They're new galoshes and they fall off my feet." I want to hurt him too. And I fling at him: "Grandpa is surely angry at you because you wouldn't recite for him."

"What else? Why are you bothering me? Instead,

tell me whom we should ride with—Ivan, or Berel the Crooked-legged? He limps on one leg, Berel does!"

"Who can see whether he limps? He sits in one spot, and certainly his horse has straight legs!"

"Why might not his horse have crooked legs too? I can believe anything about him, that scoundrel! Ha-ha-ha!"

"Master! Avreml! Little miss!" The drivers catch sight of us.

They know us. They are always standing at the corner of the street. Because of cold and boredom, they keep blowing into their hands and clapping them.

"Got your Hanukkah money?" one calls out. "How much did they give you? Come, show me! Well then, climb in, little girl!"

The drivers wrangle. One elderly driver—he seems very cold—blows a thick vapor out of his mouth, as though trying to warm himself that way. When he talks, his frozen goatee moves up and down like a hatchet chopping every word that leaves his lips. "Better come with me," he says. "Don't even think of him! Don't you see that his horse is an old jade like himself?"

"He'll put ten horses like yours inside his chest any time!" the other shouts. "May the angel of death snatch you away! You—"

The drivers never stop reviling each other.

"Come on, they're all trying to cheat you, master! You've always ridden with me! Just look, little lady, how warm you'll be under the black fur!" Ivan runs in front of all the sleighs and slides up almost against our feet.

He looks like a sack all filled up, but he bends lightly to one side, and, just as though we were his former masters, he unbuttons his worn-out sheepskin rug, and in a trice we are in his sleigh.

"Fie!" The other drivers spit. "What can you do about a devil like that!"

Ivan snaps his whip. One swish of it through the air, and the horse begins to tremble. It lifts up its tail like a cat showered with cold water.

"Giddap, you old nag, giddap!" Ivan becomes excited, he lifts himself from his seat.

The little bells ring out and then do not stop tinkling.

"Hup, hup!" goads Ivan.

Yells and lashes fly, scald the horse's cold rump like boiling water. And the steaming horse, as though trying to run away from Ivan, strains its body, heaves its flanks. Its own tail lashes it more violently than the whip. Its big legs bang against the shafts—they seem to be trying to tear off their own skin.

In the sleigh we lurch with the jolting of the horse. Now we sink in the snow, now we are tossed up high. There is no time to catch our breath. We are carried along as if we had wings.

"Come on, cholera, giddap! Huh! Ha! Hup, hup!"

Now Ivan is yelling like a madman. He whistles,

cracks his whip, roars, lifts himself up, wriggles his rump. A mountain of snow falls from his back onto us. A cloud of snow tears by at our side, chases us from behind.

Snow splashes the horse's muzzle. Its eyes are dripping with snow. Snow blankets its head, its back. Snow blows out of its nostrils, a thick steam rises from its mouth. The horse, as though it were drunk, shakes its mane, shakes the bells.

We swim behind it as in a current of water. On both sides the town flies by, one street blurs and tumbles into another. Thick snow whirls in the streets like flour spilling from sacks. Where are we? In a flash we have flown past the big city park. Only a moment ago it stood, full of trees, on a high hill— and suddenly it is gone like a snowflake in the air. And where is our big church? Who could ever move it from its place? And now it has slid by, detached itself from the ground; from its white walls there came a gust of snow, its cross had barely time to flash its gold and pierce the sky.

My cheeks are burning, stinging. I stretch out my hands, trying to snatch at some houses, streets. But everything runs away from me. Windows, shutters, signs, all are carried away by the wind, swallowed up by the snow.

We are now far from the town, as if we had flown off into the air; I no longer see anything. The frost bites us. Snow glues up my eyes, stings my eyebrows. My head is cold. Snow has got into my hair—my hair has turned hard, one could cut it with a knife. My neck is wet. My collar is full of snow.

I stamp my feet. The fur blanket has long ago become soaked with snow. It only makes me colder. My feet are like blocks of wood, there is no way of lifting them. I want to rouse Abrashke. What is the matter with him?

The wind whistles; I no longer hear my brother. Only a minute ago he was neighing like the horse. Why is there no steam coming from his mouth any longer? My face burns. Are we being frozen? Mother, mother! Where is mother? Has she run away into the sky too? She will scold: "Where are you? Where on earth have you gone off to?"

"Whoa!"

The sleigh suddenly stops, almost spilling us.

"And where are the ten kopeks?" Ivan's gruff voice rouses us.

His felt glove, thick as a bear's leg, thrusts itself before our eyes. He pulls the ten kopeks out of Abrashke's glove. His whip stuck under his belt, Ivan spits into one hand, into the other, tosses the coin as though weighing it, puts it between his teeth.

"Real silver, strong as iron!" he booms out, laughing.

"Ivan, where are we?" I ask.

"You're home, little girl, home!"

I turn around. True enough, the big church is

standing behind us, as always. Its walls, its roof, its cross, have all come back from the sky. And the sky itself has closed up, driven off the clouds. A single stray little star shines from it.

On the hill the big park has grown anew. Houses, shops, windows, everything is standing on its base again.

We crawl out of the sleigh. Where have we come riding from?

Ivan has brought us to our own big, broad street.

THE SHOP

A QUITE different world opens before me when I only just push at the heavy door that separates the shop from our apartment.

It is a door entirely covered with tin. Instead of a latch it has a big key that is always in the lock. In the dark rear shop, into which I tumble first, I grope along the walls as though I were blind. Thick yellow sheets of paper rustle underfoot.

Wrapped-up wall clocks rest on the floor here. Until they are hung on walls, they do not move; they lie quiet and soundless, as if buried alive. But the stuffy air of the dark chamber seems swollen with the voices that seep in from the shop. The voices crowd against the high wooden wall and recoil from it again. I stand behind it as in a prison, and listen to what is being said. I want to make out whose voice is talking. And if I catch mother's voice, I am content.

But wait! Is her voice quiet, calm, or, God forbid, angry? Mother's voice will give me warning, tell me whether to go into the shop or not.

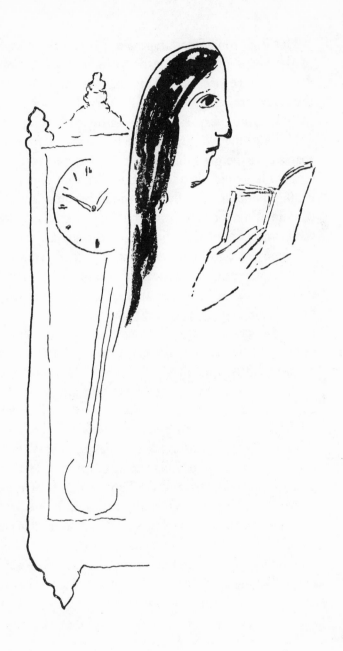

Her high tones encourage me. I touch the curtain of the last door, which leads to the shop. I become dizzy at once because of the mirrors and glass. All the clocks are being wound in my ears. The shop is full of glitter on every side. The flashing of silver and gold blinds me like fire; it is reflected in the mirrors, roams over the glass drawers. It dazzles my eyes.

Two large gas chandeliers burn high up under the ceiling, humming loudly; the sound becomes a moan of pain. Fire spatters from the close-netted caps on the burners that barely hold back the sparks.

There are two high walls entirely lined from top to bottom with glass cupboards. The cupboards reach up to the ceiling and are so solidly built that they seem to have grown into it. Their glass doors slide easily back and forth. Through the glass one can clearly see all the objects on display, almost touch them with one's hand.

On the shelves are goblets, wineglasses, sugar bowls, saucers, braided baskets, milk and water pitchers, boxes for etrogim, fruit bowls. Everything shines and glitters with a newly polished look. Whenever I move, all the objects run after me in reflection. The fire of the lamps and the light of the silver cross each other. Now the silver drowns in a flash of the lamplight, now it re-emerges with an even sharper glitter.

On the opposite wall there is another glass cupboard. Behind its panes are objects not of silver but of

white metal, and their gleam is much more modest, and quieter.

In the center of the shop, on three sides, there rise, as if from the floor itself, three inner walls—long counters with drawers. They divide the shop into two sections. All laid out with glass, full of gold objects, they glitter like magical arks. Little stones of all colors, framed in gold rings, earrings, brooches, bracelets, flicker there like lighted matches.

In this air full of fire it is quite impossible to see that the floor is dark. At the front, at the very feet of the customers, entire silver services shine through the glass. And so even the customers' black shoes glitter and catch reflections along with the silver.

The third wall is dim even by day. Overgrown with long hanging clocks, it looks like a forest of dark trees. There are wall clocks of various sizes. Some have big, squat cases with thick hanging chains supporting heavy copper weights. Other wall clocks have narrower, slimmer bodies. Their chains are lighter, more movable, with smaller weights attached. In the bellies of all of them pointed pendulums dangle like swords, swinging restlessly back and forth.

Among the large wall clocks smaller ones are hiding, and even tiny ones; one can see only the white dials, their round moon faces. They have no wooden bellies, and their chain legs move in the open, before everyone's eyes, up and down.

The whole wall of clocks sighs and breathes heavily. From each box come smothered groans, as though at every moment someone were being killed on the dark wall.

Suddenly I begin to quake. One of the heavy clocks awakens, and, like an old man rousing, it utters such a groan that I look around quickly to see whether its body has fallen apart.

Heavily it strikes the hours. My heart pounds with its heart. And I am glad when the minute hand moves away a bit from the hour hand, giving me time to catch my breath before the old thing utters another groan.

Another clock acts as though it were blowing its nose, or hoarsely rending its throat in broken laughter.

In contrast, the little clocks have high, thin little voices. They wail like children awakened in terror in the middle of the night.

The clocks move, their pendulums swing, for days and nights on end. When do they rest?

Suddenly several clocks together begin to chime. Do they do it on purpose, in order not to let me hear how each one sounds by itself?

I turn my head from one clock to another. I am bewildered. I hear voices that seem to come straight from the earth.

These are the little alarm clocks lying on the floor in cardboard boxes. Like clamoring brats they awaken the old wall clocks.

I rush to twist their little heads in order to make them stop yelling. But I stop halfway. My heart melts. A gentle song rises on the air. I know that it is a music box that is singing. I quickly open its lid. The song flies out like a bird from its nest. In the box there surges a sea of little wires, springs, wheels. Like waves they lift tiny millstones, jump over them, quickly run down, swim in the melody as in the current of a stream. Each little spring, each little wheel breaks into sound. They hum the melody till they lose their breath.

I go quite close to the music box; I want to assure it that someone is listening, that it must not stop playing. But suddenly the little wheels stop. I do not close the lid. I wait—perhaps it will want to sing again.

Such a warm world has risen from the dark one and spread over the whole shop! Even the wall clocks are holding their breath.

Every night, before going to sleep, one of my brothers goes to have a look at the shop. My parents send him to see whether everything is in order, whether, God forbid, a burglar has not broken in. I too want to see how all the objects on display sleep there at night.

As soon as the big key of the metal door creaks, I shudder. I am afraid to go there, even with my brother. What if the angel of death with all his devils were concealed there?

But they have a little light. A small table lamp burns there overnight. The wick is twisted. The smoke of the smothered flame drags out our shadows, whirls them before my eyes.

A smoky veil covers also the wall with the shelves of silver. Only here and there, a sleepy eye seems to open—a carved flower sparkles, a raised ornament flickers; suddenly a full glow of silver light shines forth, like the moon rolling out from behind the clouds.

I am afraid to go closer to the wall of the clocks. They hang on black nails, as though eternally crucified. It seems to me that open graves sigh there. The clocks are barely moving, their pendulums drag like limping feet. The white dials with their black dots wink with faded eyes, like specters.

I hear them from a distance and help them to sigh. It seems to me that they are calling me, that they are prodding me in the back. With a heavy heart I leave them.

I see that in our apartment, in our dining room, there is also a wall clock, but it is enclosed inside a high, carved cabinet. One does not hear its heart pound, one does not see its outstretched legs. It strikes the hours with a muffled tone that has no spirit.

PURIM GIFTS

A WHITE snow, a pale sun. With the early morning Purim has come. A thin frost has carved
white horses with heroic riders on the window panes.
A little wind brings the tidings: today is a holiday!

My brother Abrashke and I have run to meet it.
We received Purim money. The copper coins clinked
in our hands. We ran to the meat market on the
square. We found it already full of stir like a fair.

The old, dilapidated tables were blanketed with
white hole-riddled tablecloths, as with snow blown
in. The tables were set as for a wedding. Women and
children stamped around the tables, as the men do
in shul during the ceremony of hakkafot. The tables
were dazzling, bewitching.

A whole world of little beings of frozen candy was
spread on the tables. Little horses, sheep, birds, dolls,
and cradles—their red-yellow dots seemed to wink at
us, to show that they were still alive, that they were
not yet quite dead. Little golden fiddles looked as
though they had fallen asleep while playing a last

melody. Mordecais and Ahasueruses on horseback seemed to be raising themselves in the saddle.

The cold sun occasionally cast his rays on all these dreamlike Purim gifts and hardly warmed their coats of sugar. Abrashke and I elbowed up close to the tables, as if we were trying to rescue the frozen toys with our own breath. We wanted to take them all with us. On the street here, wouldn't they be frozen to death?

"Children, let's get on with it! Choose your presents and go home!" The freezing vendor interrupted our dreams.

As though it were easy to choose! Our hearts pounded. We looked at the Purim toys, hoping that they themselves would tell us which of them wanted to go with us, which to remain.

How could one let them go out of one's hands? And what should we take? A big horse or a small one? My friend Zlatke might think that in giving her the bigger horse I wanted to show off, yet she would be more pleased with it than with the smaller one. So I touched the little horse in front and in back.

"Bashke, what are you doing? It's dangerous to touch it!" my brother teased me.

I let go of the horse, as though I feared that it might bite me. My teeth were chattering, either from cold or from the temptation of the thought whispering to me that all these little horses and little violins were the sweetest of all sweets, and that it would feel

[164]

good to be crunching them alive in one's mouth.

"If you wish, I'll deliver your Purim presents," said a tall, scrawny boy coming up to us.

"Sure, yes—come with us!"

His round, sad eyes, the eyes of a much-beaten dog, drew us after him. And like a dog he ran in front of us.

"What's your name?" we asked him.

"Pinye."

Pinye? That is a strange name, like a bird's.

"Can you whistle?"

At home we spread our Purim gifts on two plates, one plate for Abrashke and the other for me.

The little sugar animals seemed to come back to life in the warm air. Their little cheeks began to glisten. Frightened, I blew on them, so that they should not melt from the heat. That would be the last straw—that our presents should melt, fall apart in little bits. More than once we changed the plates, picked among the presents, sorted them. I clung particularly to the little candy violin. It nestled in my fingers, stroked them, like a toy bow, as if it were trying to play a melody on them.

"And if I send the little violin to my friend, it will surely never come back to me," I thought, feeling a stab in my heart.

But Pinye, the errand boy, was shuffling his feet, waiting for our presents. Trembling with emotion, we gazed for the last time on our plates, wrapped them each in a kerchief, and gathered together the corners.

"Pinye, see, here are our Purim gifts. But you mustn't run, mind you! Better walk slowly! You must not—God forbid—slip on the wet snow with the plates. And don't turn around! You might be pushed! What is the matter, are you asleep? Why do you look at us as in a dream?" And we shook the boy by his shoulders.

Pinye started from his place and at once began to run. The plates shook in his hands.

"Don't rush like that, Pinye! Have you no time? What's the hurry? Watch out, hold fast to the corners of the kerchiefs!" we shouted after him.

Oh, he'll make trouble, that boy, I said to myself. He has such long legs! Our presents will tumble over on one another. And suppose an ear of the horse breaks off on the way, or the top of the curved little violin falls off? What will our friends think? That we sent them broken presents?

"Where are you, Pinye?"

But Pinye has vanished.

Right now, I keep thinking, Pinye has turned into the little street where my friend Zlatke lives. The black latch of the door is lifted from inside, and from behind the door Zlatke appears, as though she had been waiting for the messenger.

"Are the two for me?" And Zlatke stretches out both hands.

"No, this one is yours!" And Pinye probably confuses our plates.

Zlatke snatches the little plate from Pinye's hands and runs to her bedroom. Pinye remains standing there.

In the kitchen, Zlatke's mother is busying herself. With a long iron fork she lifts a big black pot and pushes it into the oven. Pinye's tongue hangs out of his mouth. He wants to eat. The roasted meat and potatoes smell so good.

"Zlatke, why does it take so long? Have you fallen asleep there, or what? Ai, what children get excited about! Going wild over nothing!"

Zlatke's mother turns to the boy with a cry. "What are you standing for, you ninny? For the same money you can sit down!"

Zlatke is somewhat fat, with short little legs, and she wears her hair in a long, heavy pigtail on her back. And she always walks so slowly that I get bored looking at her. Even her big eyes stare as if frozen in her face. Before she gets through with the Purim gifts, the Messiah himself might come. She probably examines my plate from all sides, touches the little horse and the golden lamb. She puts them to her nose, to her ears.

Her long pigtail wiggles on her back as though it were helping her to think. She is unable to fix her attention on anything. And suppose Zlatke wants to keep the whole plate?

[167]

Oh, why do I think up such false accusations? I shame myself. Probably Zlatke runs to the drawer where she keeps her own presents, spreads out her little horses and lambs, and compares them with mine.

"She is taking the sweet little violin from my plate!" I think with pounding heart.

And what will she put in its place? Oh, why doesn't the boy come back? He has vanished as though forever! I begin to question Abrashke: "Do you think Pinye has already been at my friend's?"

But my brother teases me. He thinks that being older than I, and a boy to boot, he can make fun of me. So he bursts into laughter.

Let him laugh, by all means! I know nevertheless that he too is waiting for Pinye, that he is dying to see what has remained on his plate, and what gifts for him have been added on it. To whom is he boasting? Don't I see that he keeps looking out of the window, watching for the return of our Pinye?

"You know, Bashke," he says, "Pinye probably won't be back for at least an hour. You know that my friend Motke lives on the other side of the river. And by the time that dreamy Pinye crosses the bridge, we shall be falling asleep. How can you expect him not to stop to have a look at what is going on in the river? Perhaps the ice has begun to break!"

And what if Abrashke is right? I am bursting with grief.

"Pinye is capable of anything," I agree with my

brother. "That's all he has to do—inspect the whole river! He won't even be back for the meal!"

"You dumb cluck, you believe everything! I've just made that up!" My brother is now rolling with laughter.

Suddenly he pushes me to one side and like a cat scrambles down all the stairs that lead to the kitchen. Pinye is knocking at the door.

"Ah, you brats, why do you make so much noise?" the fat cook yells at us. "You idlers! All day long you roam about here—you don't give me a chance to do anything. Out of the kitchen!"

We drag Pinye into the house. First we look into his eyes, then into the plates. He has probably seen what kind of presents have been sent us in exchange for ours.

Well, the little violin must be gone! I read it in Pinye's sad eyes. I open the kerchief on my plate. Yes, she did take the pretty little violin! And I have no other violin, and I don't need the doll she has given me. I've got two like it. Abrashke has given me his. And that's what made her fuss for a whole hour! In anger I bite my lips.

What? He is laughing again, Abrashke, and even that silly Pinye too! I can't look at them any more.

Abrashke is lucky. He can afford to be in a good mood. Motke has put a big horse on his plate. In his enthusiasm, Abrashke neighs like a real horse.

Weeping, I run to the kitchen.

"Why do you make such a long face?" The cook throws the words at me while chopping onions. "What is the matter, did you get a bad Purim gift?" And she keeps on babbling in her usual fashion, as though she were chopping the onions with her tongue, and she spatters me with wet crumbs. "What a misfortune that is! May you have no greater grief until your hundred-and-twentieth year! Silly girl, you'll surely forget about it before your wedding!"

Whether because of the onions or because of her words, my eyes begin actually to drop tears.

"Here, take your little Haman-tash." And the cook squeezes into my hands a triangular cake, bursting with heat and with the poppyseed with which it is stuffed.

My hands at once become wet and warm as though somebody had kissed them.

"You see, Bashutke, there was no reason for crying!" Sasha cheers me with her smile. "You know what? Just wait a while—when I'm through with my work, I'll run out for a minute and exchange your doll for a violin."

"Darling Sasha!" I creep into her skirts, stuffed underneath like a whole wardrobe, and wipe my eyes on her sleeves.

"That's enough, Bashutke, go now, let me work! It will be mealtime soon! Why do you keep spinning around me, you crazy girl?" And she pushes me away gently.

In the dark rear shop I bump into something hard. Aha, a woven basket! This must be mother's Purim gifts prepared for our uncles and aunts. A basket packed full of good things! How can mother send them away so improvidently? The basket will have bottles of red and white wine, bottles of sweet syrups, big pears, wooden boxes with cigars heaped on one another like blocks; there will be cans of sprats and sardines, and amidst all this a new red tablecloth with painted flowers.

Mother has been busy in the shop, as always, and probably has forgotten her Purim presents. Doesn't she even think of them? The basket will soon be carried away! And isn't she waiting at all for the presents that she will get?

I imagine my good Aunt Rachel's delight over mother's presents: "Lord of the Universe! So many good things! And all that for me! Ah, Alta, you'll spoil me altogether!"

My aunt's weak heart is choked with joy. She sniffs at the basket; she seems instantly to be made drunk by all the good smells, for she closes her eyes. Then she awakens as if from a dream. She feels the tablecloth, lifts it in the air, strokes it. She might be saying a benediction: "Thank you, Altinke! May God in heaven grant you many healthful and happy years! How could you guess so truly? I really needed a new tablecloth for Pesach, to honor my guests."

And suddenly my aunt fancies that a speck of dust

has fallen on the new tablecloth. She blows away the speck, and fearing that the tablecloth may become soiled before the Passover, she carefully lays it in its folds.

How many baskets with presents have been carried through the streets from one house to another! And the things they were filled with! The scrawny woman messengers were hardly able to hold them up.

"Is Itchke at home?"

I suddenly hear an unfamiliar voice in the kitchen. In the doorway stands a little old Jewish woman, wrapped in a big shawl. In her hands she holds a yellowed candy horse as one holds a little live chicken.

"Bashinke, gut yom-tov!" And she smiles at me with her thin lips. "Is Itchke in? There's a Purim present for him!"

She lifts the little horse. She wants to show me how big and beautiful her present is. And indeed, the little horse almost seems to be bigger and fatter than she is.

A strange woman, like someone just out of a mad-house. Was she really once my brother Itchke's nurse? Now he is tall and big—how could he have had this little woman for a nurse?

My brother has for many years been living abroad, studying medicine, but the old woman comes every Purim to bring him a gift. The dried-up nurse always explains that she wants to have a look at her Itchke.

Mother presses a silver coin into her hand and tells

her in a low voice, as though fearing to frighten her, that Itchke is not at home, and that she can take back her little horse: the present may come in handy next year, God willing. And actually the little horse grows yellower and yellower every year.

One day the old woman found Itchke at home. But when she saw in the doorway a grown-up young man, she was so frightened that she ran out of the kitchen as if someone were chasing her. She even forgot to hand him the little horse.

No one stopped her. And since then she has not returned.

Mother distributes gifts among the people she employs in the house and in the shop. Something glistens in her fingers. A pair of golden earrings and a ring stick out from their tissue paper—presents for the maids. At every holiday they receive golden things. And they are happy to think that they are collecting jewelry, although they have never married.

I look at our bookkeeper. Usually quiet, wordless, he now becomes talkative and his mustache quivers. His hands stroke a new silver watch.

Huneh, the clerk, quietly folds a white silken kerchief that mother has given him for his young wife.

Unlike him, Rose, the salesgirl, fills the shop with her loud enthusiasm, turns about before the mirror, boasts to everyone of her beautiful medallion, her Purim present. The cashier has received some money.

Although she is busy all day long with a box full of money, she has found herself short of funds.

The watchmaker receives some bottles of wine—he has enough watches in his table drawer. The faces of all of them are radiant, as though a wedding were being celebrated in the shop.

"Close the shop! It will soon be dinnertime!" Father's voice breaks into the noisy gathering.

THE BOOK OF ESTHER

A<small>FTER</small> the heavy frosts, winter suddenly withdraws. The snow caves in. The ice loses its luster. Winds arrive with new odors from far-off places and drive away the cold.

With the winds, Purim pushes closer. It comes knocking at our door.

One night, a tall scrawny Jew comes in and stands in the kitchen doorway, like an exhausted messenger from afar. His face is buried under hair. His black beard is all tangled. Apparently no wind was able to blow through its thick tufts. His forelocks, like little braids, reach down from under his cap to fall into his beard. His eyebrows, thick, bristling, overhang his deep, sunken little eyes like a gabled roof.

Panting, the newcomer stands in the doorway. His beard breathes with him. His big nose, curved like a horn, blows at his mustache, at his beard, as though trying to air them at least a little bit.

"Look, Reb Laib is here!" the stranger says.

The cook turns to him.

"Oi, woe is me, and my Haman-tashen are still in

the oven!" She quickly wipes her hands, throws down her greasy apron, and puts on a pious holiday face.

The man in the doorway is not a beggar who has come to ask for alms. It is Reb Laib in the flesh, the megillah reader, who has entered the kitchen.

Every Purim he comes to read the Book of Esther to us in our house. That is to say, he reads it to mother, to me, and to the cook. For the shop is open, and mother has no time to go to listen to the reading of the Book of Esther in shul.

"Why are you standing in the doorway, Reb Laib?" Havah is happy because she can exchange a word with a pious Jew and show him that she is pious too. "Come in! The mistress is waiting for you. Well, thank God, we have lived to see Purim! May the All-Highest bestow a miracle every year, may he thus save us from all our sufferings!"

She suddenly sobs. The visitor, embarrassed, blinks his eyes. Perhaps he is late?

Havah grows more voluble. For a moment it seems to her that the reader has come for her sake, to tell her a good long story. "Sit down, Reb Laib!" she says. "All the time on one's feet! One is no longer a human being that way!"

She pushes up a chair for him. Her own feet are always swollen, and she thinks only of sitting down.

The man remains standing as though she were not addressing him. He does not even look at her. His eyes are lowered, and he has caught a hair of his beard in his mouth and is chewing it. His long, thin legs are bent under him. He stands leaning on them as on a stick.

The whole year round, no one sees him. On the eve of Purim he looks so tired out that he seems to have roamed all over the world from Purim to Purim. Does he tell everyone about the miracle of Purim, or does he look for new miracles in order to be able to recount them to us along with the story of Esther?

He takes a pinch of snuff, begins to cough, draws his red handkerchief from his pocket, wipes his mouth, and as though he were closing it with his fingers, he finally removes his hand.

"May you be spared from the evil eye, Bashinke," he says, winking at me, "you've grown a good deal during the year! Have you got your rattle? This year you'll be strong enough to outshout Haman all by yourself, eh?" With every word he speaks his mustache jumps up and his long yellow teeth stick out of his mouth, like the yellow keys of an old piano.

I run to mother in the shop, calling her: "Mother, mother, come quickly! The man has come to read the Book of Esther to us!"

"Really? Is it as late as that?" She immediately leaves all the hubbub of the shop. "Children, keep an eye on the unpacked merchandise! I'll be back soon. Huneh, see to it that no child leaves the shop, will you?" She quickly throws instructions to the employees and hurries out.

I run after her. "Mother, do you know where the rattle is? The man is asking for it. I'm supposed to outshout Haman!"

"Ah, let me alone! You're always bothering me with questions. If you can't get your rattle, you can stamp your feet."

Upon seeing mother, the visitor stirs from his place. "Good evening, good evening, Alta!" And he wags his head.

"Good evening, good evening, come in, Reb Laib! It must be late, isn't it? I suppose they've finished reciting the book at the shul, eh?"

Instead of answering, he smiles shyly into his beard and goes by us with stooped shoulders, in order not to touch us, God forbid. As soon as he has passed us, he advances through the apartment with huge strides, as though he were in the street.

"Bashinke, here is your rattle!" Havah pants into my ear and pushes a wooden Purim rattle into my hand.

"But it's last year's," I protest. "It's no good. It doesn't rattle any more!"

"May all my enemies be stricken as hard as you can strike with this to deafen Haman! You'll see, Reb Laib will tell you the same thing."

The megillah reader has stopped at the bookcase; he opens its two doors wide and thrusts in his hand, long as a shovel. Without looking he grasps from out of some corner the scroll that he tucked away there a

year ago. The quiet bookcase rocks, and several books are scattered to one side. As though in anger, they give off a little cloud of dust.

Reb Laib catches up the scroll and carries it like a treasure. The white silken cover of the scroll, its embroidered golden letters, its crowns, cast a sunny light on the reader's dark face. Even his beard becomes transparent. Revived, cheered, he goes to the table. He does not even cast a glance at us. He removes his cap. His black velvet skullcap adds more luster to him. On his shoulders his short talis spreads like a pair of white wings.

"Silence!" He bangs with his hand. He probably imagines that he is about to recite in a shul packed full of people.

"Silence!" He bangs the table again, although the three of us are standing there in utter quiet.

He gathers his strength. He bows to the scroll, kisses it, removes its cover. And like Samson pushing at the pillars of the temple, he leans on the handles of the scroll and unrolls it. A musty smell comes from the yellow scroll as he unfurls it wide. A little heap of black lines arrayed in equal rows like stairs stands up on the table. Reb Laib raises his head, cranes his long, gooselike neck.

"Ho-ho! Ah-ah!" He makes a gargling sound and clears his voice.

The chandelier shines in his face. He stares into the light. As though he had absorbed its fire, his face lights up. He sways to one side, to the other, and then, in a high, chanting voice, he sings out the first benedictions of the scroll. All three of us repeat them aloud.

The reader, once set going, does not stop. Harnessed to the table, leaning on the scroll, he rocks his body as if someone were prodding him. The stiff parchment rustles in his hands. A noise arises around him.

I imagine that the entire array of lines has begun to move and that they are whirling as on wheels.

Here is King Ahasuerus coming down from his castle. A whole host of soldiers is thronging after him; they ride over the lines, trample upon the letters—the words might be little pebbles under the horses' feet.

The reader hurries, recites at a fast pace. In one breath he takes a whole heap of the letters into his mouth. Ahasuerus and his soldiers are pursuing him; each word is a step he gains on them.

He crumples the pages, tears out the lines, and tosses them high on his throbbing voice. Each line is drawn out with the melody as though it were threaded on a string. Now he drags it upward, now he tosses it out and brings it back all curled up. Then once again he swallows a few lines, and the same melody drags them up and down. He seems to veil the whole story in a trembling cloud.

Only from time to time does he force his voice; perhaps he hopes that thus he can push Ahasuerus himself. We listen to him with bated breath. I try to see the king riding by and the moment when Mordecai arrives on his white horse.

Mother holds her translated text in her hand, and as if she were checking the reader, keeps nodding her head. Havah the cook, huddling in the doorway, sighs and snaps her fingers. "It's true, everything he says is true!" her lips whisper.

I look into the reader's mouth. I cannot keep up with his fast-moving tongue, which knocks like a little hammer against his teeth. I cannot reach the place in the text at which he is reciting. Now he is on this side of a page, and then the page is already rolled up, and his eyes have jumped to the next page.

I can hardly wait for the word Haman to come. God forbid that I should miss it! For I must outshout Haman all alone. The rattle is sweating in my hands— God knows whether it will rattle properly.

I move closer to the scroll. I touch its silver handles. They bar me off from the yellow parchment like two big pillars. Just such pillars, I think to myself, must be standing at the entrance of the king's castle. They will light up the path for Esther. In a moment she will come forth in her long dress, with her long, golden hair. And in fact the lines are now more widely spaced; a wide square opens up. Now her radiant face appears.

Suddenly Reb Laib gives me a push. He probably wants to push me out of the queen's way. I look at him angrily. But his neck is craned up to the very ceiling. Like a thunderclap, his voice crashes out: "Haman, Haman, the son of Hammedatha!"

Mother and Havah stamp their feet.

Why did I have to get lost in a dream about Esther at just this point! I have hardly had a chance to shake my Haman rattle. Annoyed, I bang it on the table.

Reb Laib catches his breath and plunges into the story again. I no longer take my eyes off him.

"Haman, Haman!" He nods to me—he seems to be trying to indicate to me that Haman has run out of the scroll and that I am to hit him, kill him on the spot.

I bang my rattle on the table, I stamp my feet, I yell. If Haman should get away from me, mother or Havah must catch him.

"Haman! Haman!" the reader now cries out with each minute, as though not one but a thousand Hamans had crept out of the scroll.

The din of our voices becomes fearful. The reader rolls the scroll noisily. Page groans after page. What if we don't manage to kill Haman? Will he strike us through with his drawn sword? Where are you, Esther? Hurry, hurry! Perform your miracle!

And actually, Reb Laib stops shouting, stops swaying, as though Esther were shining on him from the newly unrolled page of the scroll. He softens his voice, adorns the chant as though with delicate flowers, and bows, bows, as if he were trying to stroke Esther's robe.

[183]

"Mother, thank God, Esther has come!" I whisper to mother.

All of us feel relief in our hearts. Mother utters a sigh. Havah's eyes are raised—she seems to be praising God for having shown his mercy in time.

And under the reader's chant Esther walks down the stairs of spaced lines. Her long train glistens, spreads over the empty place on which there is not a single letter but only white ribbons of light, as though white candles had been lit on the scroll in honor of the holiday.

"Amen! Amen!" we chant with the reader.

The melody has run out, and Reb Laib is silent. His hands remain resting on the scroll. I am standing and waiting—perhaps something more will issue from his closed mouth, from his beard, which has suddenly turned black. But there is only silence, as though something had died.

The reader quietly kisses the scroll on both its sides, just as if they were cheeks, and brings its handles tightly together. The scroll becomes old, thin. Reb Laib takes it to the bookcase. We accompany it with our eyes. We know that we shall not see it again for a whole year.

Coming back from the bookcase, the reader suddenly stops and looks at us with his big eyes, and says: "So only you three have heard me?"

It seemed to him that he had recited the megillah to the whole world.

THE PURIM PLAYERS

THROUGH the whole day of Purim our house is in
an uproar. Up until the hour of the feast there is a
continual wrapping up and carrying away of gifts.
Here a basket is being filled with good things; there
packages sent by relatives are being unwrapped.

The old woman porter has no strength left. "Believe me," she wails, "I have lost the use of my hands
and feet!" Sighing deeply, she places on the table the
basket she has brought, cracks her knuckles, and sits
down.

"Dvoshe, you'll rest for a whole year," says the
cook. "Go, there is another basket to be taken—but
hurry, for it will be time for the dinner soon!" The
cook does not permit her to catch her breath.

In the dining room the chandelier is lighted. The
samovar is brought in, gleaming and bubbling more
than ever.

Having closed the shop, mother runs into the apartment. "Where is Dvoshe?" she asks. Then she recalls
suddenly. "Has she taken the gifts to everyone? To
Aunt Zipe? And my elder sister-in-law? Do you re-

member the bad experience we had with her last year? Think well—you haven't forgotten anyone?"

The old porter—the same woman serves each year—knows mother's relatives by heart. "With God's help, Alta," she says, "I've taken the gifts to all, and all were happy with your gifts, and wished you even more than they have put in the baskets!"

"Well, then, Dvoshe, here is your own Purim gift—have a good holiday!" And mother squeezes a few coins into her hand.

"Thanks, Altinke! May you too have a good and cheerful holiday. Let us live in good health and good luck to see the next Purim, God willing!"

Father sits at the table in his long silken coat. His beard is brushed, each hair of it is fluffed. His face is shining under the sparkling chandelier light. From its flame, little balls of light scatter over the tablecloth. Wherever they jump, a bit of the table is illumined. On one side mother's tall candles flare up. The holiday table is prepared for the feast.

The shames comes in. The gabbai, and a neighbor whose house is on the courtyard, follow him. They come to wish father a happy holiday. Father asks them all to table: "Sit down, Reb Efraim! Sit down, Reb David! Take a glass of tea while we wait for dinner!"

So they sit and drink tea as though it were wine. With each glass they grow more lively, and after each glass they melt with heat and pleasure.

[186]

On the table, at father's hand, there lies ready a little heap of silver and copper coins. For each beggar who enters the house, father shoves up a little mound of change.

"A merry holiday to you, Reb Shmul Noah! A gut yom-tov, baleboste!" each of them says, bowing his head.

The door never closes. We might as well be sitting in the street with the people walking by us. All of the poor people of the town pass through our house.

A tall man with a black beard comes up to father and stands before him. I imagine that King Ahasuerus in person has come: at any moment all of us will rise from our seats, even father, and yield him the place at the head of the table. But the man goes away, not at all like a king, but with lowered head.

The heap of money grows smaller and smaller. Who else is to come? For whom is father waiting?

Suddenly the glasses on the table quiver. A noise comes from the kitchen, as though people were fighting there, as though plates and silver were dropping on the floor. There is jostling, laughter. Feet are stamping. Men are whistling, laughing. Father and the guests exchange glances.

"These must be the Purim players!" the shames whispers.

The door flies open with a bang, and a whole company of people stumbles in—tall ones, small ones, fat ones, thin ones. They seem to be not only pushing in

from the door but also creeping out from the walls, from every corner. They have burst open all the doors and windows.

From everywhere people are popping out. One has

a monstrous nose, another a pair of swollen cheeks. And there is a head like a blue sugar cone. And no feet are to be seen.

Where are their feet? And they do not stand in one place. One climbs on top of another, nudges him in the side, trips him, falls down himself, dragging the other, and the two roll over. We burst into laughter.

"Sha!" Out of the hurlyburly comes a tall fellow with a red cardboard nose that he holds with his hand and tries to paste to his face. Probably his own nose is even uglier and that is why he conceals it!

"Gut yom-tov, Yehudim! Gut yom-tov, my hosts! Here comes the merry Purim, the red nose!" And he suddenly begins to whistle through his big nostrils. Father and the guests nod their heads.

"Gut yom-tov!" all the Purim players repeat in a chant. Red Nose becomes excited.

"Company of musicians!" he commands. "Why have you stopped? Let us all make merry, dance!" And he begins to sing, stamp his feet, clap his hands; his boots thump like hammers on the floor.

All of them whirl around the room. They all seem drunk; they tumble, they turn somersaults. Each wants to distinguish himself, show off as many tricks as possible.

"Where are you, Mendl the Drum!" one loud voice outshouts all the rest.

A fat stuffed figure of a drum comes forward. This is Mendl. It is as though he had no legs. Behind him trots a pair of legs that do not belong to him. A long hand comes out from one side and bangs the drum on its belly; from behind his ears a pair of brass cymbals creep out and crash against his head, slapping his cheeks.

Now a trumpet booms, now a horn blows, now a pipe whistles, and noise bursts out of all of them.

They seem to be whirling right over my head. I no longer know where to look first. I fancy that they are crying out in anger at the man with the red nose. He pushes them all around, does not let anyone play out his own trick.

"Quiet!" he yells. "Here comes King Ahasuerus!"

And he himself steps forward, takes off his red nose, and puts a golden crown on his head. Always he!

"Perhaps he'll also play Esther, with his big boots?" the others murmur.

One of the company cuts across his path. He is riding on a white stick.

"I am Mordecai!" he cries, and at this point another actor, wearing a pointed tin head, shakes the little bells attached to his cap; they tinkle in everyone's ears.

It is as though bells hung not only on his cap, but even on his feet, on his whole body. Father cannot stand it any longer; he holds his ears and then wipes his eyes, which are wet from laughter.

"Ha-ha-ha!" laughs the fat gabbai, and his belly

shakes. "He has come a bit too early, he has stopped the king instead of Haman!"

"Enough, enough!" Father stops them all. "You surely still have to get around to all the rest of the town!" His hand scrapes across the table.

Red Nose leaps nimbly—he is King Ahasuerus—and snatches all the money that flies off the table. The company becomes even more excited. Now they are fighting in earnest. Father's voice separates them. "Alta, have some drinks served!" he calls.

A glass of brandy is poured for each. Each swallows it in one gulp, almost with the glass. Something like a fire bursts out in them. They revel, they dance. Eyes sparkle, the drum booms, the pipes whistle, the cymbals clash, the feet stamp, the bells tinkle, tinkle. They call, they tug, they pull all of us away. My head swims. I rush toward them, and all of a sudden —what's that?

The bells sound less and less, they are quieter and quieter—farther and farther away, as if I myself were far from them. I turn around. The Purim players are not there—they have all thronged out through the door. All the sounds run after them—now one, now another. They trickle away.

Where are the Purim players? They seem to have vanished, as though they had never been. In our house it is silent, much more silent than before. Only the chandelier sputters fire, tries to keep up the holiday.

Drinks are served. The table is set. New guests

arrive. I look at the door to see whether the Purim players are not coming back. "Father," I ask, "where are the Purim players? Where have they run to? Are they dancing somewhere? Or are they now walking in the streets like other people?"

Father looks around him, smiling with the guests. "Is it time to start dinner, eh?" he calls out.

They all rise from their seats. I follow them, and in my ears the bells are still tinkling.

DINNERTIME

"SASHA, Havah, have you fallen asleep in the kitchen, or what?" cries Israel from the dining room. "Don't you hear that I'm home?"

He always grumbles, my brother Israel. He is stubborn. He is angry when he is slighted, when the best portion is given to another. He sits at the table, toys for a moment with his fork over his plate, then suddenly shoves it aside. "Look at the piece of meat you've given me!" he says. "Just bare bones, nothing to eat on it!"

A murmur comes from the kitchen, closer and closer, along with Havah's heavy steps. She pours on my brother a hail of words: "Why do you all set upon me? Why are you trying to shorten my years? Everyone sucks my blood!"

Havah shakes all over her body. Her face is red as a beet. She is not afraid of the children of the household. And she yells: "You're not an only son here! Look at this aristocrat! Is it my fault that you come later than anyone? It's always, 'Havah, Havah, I want a veal schnitzel! Havah, I want a sweet-sour

kaikele! Havah, I want roasted potatoes with prunes!'
One wants a pancake—of all things—another wants
meat, still another milk dishes!"

Havah apes each of us. She grimaces and spits.
"And if you don't satisfy them! They tear things out
of my hands, the brats! I have a hard time keeping
something for the master and mistress!" She clutches
her heart; her chest rises and falls. Suddenly she stops,
compresses her fat lips, and makes a face. "And perhaps you think that I've eaten all the meat? God is
my witness!" She holds her belly. "As though I could
eat anything with my sick stomach," she wails, and
squeezes out a tear. "A whole household is persecut-
ing me!" she goes on. "Toiling like a horse! If at
least someone had pity on me!"

"All right, all right, we've heard enough from
you!" My brother Israel is not moved by her tears.
"Better go and attend to your things in the kitchen
and bring me another piece of meat," he says, pushing
his plate into her hands. "And don't forget," he calls
after her, "change my kasha and honey, it's cold
now!"

On weekdays each of us eats separately. Sitting
alone at table, one does not know what to do with
oneself. For whole days my brothers go about idly.
But each of them wants to show the maids that he too
is important, just as busy as father and mother, and
that like them he has no time to lose while being
served.

And it is true that mother has no time for eating. She is in the shop from morning on. She waits till father and all the help come back from dinner, and when it becomes a little quieter in the shop, she snatches a moment to run to the apartment and take a bit of food.

It is only on an occasional happy day, a day without grief, that mother does not begrudge herself a meal on time. Usually she comes back to the apartment late, care-ridden and toilworn. And then it is better not to bother her.

She runs through the rear shop where the bookkeeper sits. She does not even look at him—seems to feel ashamed that she goes to sit at table in the middle of the day.

"Sasha, is there anything to eat?" she calls from a distance. "Hurry, hurry, put everything on the table! But do it quickly, I have no time!"

The harried maid quickly clears a corner of the table for mother, puts bread, salt, and a spoon and a fork before her. While mother washes and dries her hands, she goads the maid: "My God, why does everything take so long with you? Sasha, where have you vanished to? Have the children had their dinner? Has Bashke eaten anything?" She suddenly remembers me.

About the boys, she is sure that they will not let themselves be cheated by the cook. As for me, always a pale little girl, and her youngest child moreover, she always thinks that I have to be forcibly fed.

Everything is now on the table, and Sasha pushes the dish of soup toward mother. "It's a pity, barinke," Sasha says with regret. "The meat will get cold by the time you've finished your soup!"

Mother sits on the edge of the chair listening to the distant voices coming from the shop. "You silly woman," she chides, "don't make my head turn! My brain is bursting without anything from you. Be quiet for a moment, I can hear that someone has come to the shop."

Now mother is ready to run away, and hurriedly swallows the bite of food in her mouth.

"Baleboste, the balebos is asking for you!" says the panting shop boy, running in.

Mother jumps up from her seat at once. The maid looks at her sadly, and asks: "Shall I serve your food in the shop, barinke?"

I am alone at the table. There is no one who could report to mother that I don't eat. I say to the maid, who keeps placing one dish after another on the table: "Sasha, I don't want to eat!"

"Bashutke, God be with you! What are you saying? But it's so tasty! Don't you smell it? Just try it, you'll see that it will make all your limbs melt! Bashinke, what's the matter with you? You're not sick, God forbid? Just wait, I'll call Havah."

She knows that I am more afraid of Havah than of her. In comes the cook, who always smells of onion.

"Why don't you want to eat?" she assails me at once. "Ah, please, don't make such a fuss! When will you be sensible and eat like everyone else? You don't eat, and that's why you're so pale, and then your mother will again accuse me of not giving you enough to eat!"

"All right, all right, I'll eat—only stop bothering me!" I bite off a piece of meat only to make her go away. I cannot stand her smell of onion and dishwater.

"O me! Lord of the Universe! Even a tiny child turns against me!" Havah shrugs her shoulders, wipes her perpetually teary eyes with her greasy apron, and goes back to the kitchen.

I sit alone again. I swallow a bite, I look at the door hoping that someone, no matter who, will come in. And I count how many days remain before the Sabbath. On the Sabbath all the empty chairs will move toward the table, and father, mother, my brothers will sit on them.

Suddenly the door opens and Abrashke flies in like a wind. "You dumb cluck, why are you sitting here like a sleeping devil? See, there's the ice cream vendor!" And he pushes me to the window.

We stand petrified. In the courtyard a tall goy is walking about like a living white mountain. He looks as if he were blanketed with snow. He wears a loose white shirt. On his head, like another head, a high tub sways, wrapped in white cloth. The goy's face cannot be seen. It looks as though his own head were enveloped in cold towels because it hurt him.

The goy strides with his long, strong legs, trampling on the snow. He takes a step. His black, shining boots dance, and the tub on his head keeps time. Suddenly he comes to a halt opposite our window. Probably he has caught sight of us. And he cranes his neck and crows like a cock before rain: "I-i-ice crea-eam! Ice crea-eam!"

Even the window begins to shake. Abrashke jumps from the window to the door and back, and falls upon me: "Why are you standing here? Go ask mother for five kopeks! The goy refuses to give us any more credit!"

"Mother is busy, I'm afraid."

"You idiot, go at least and order the glasses!"

He himself runs to the kitchen, charges the cook from behind, and pushes her to the window to see for herself that the ice cream man is there. "Havah"— and he keeps shaking her—"you must give us five kopeks. You see that the ice cream man has come."

"O me, Lord of the Universe! He is killing me, the bandit!" And she pushes my brother away. "Are you crazy, out of your mind? An ague, that's what I'll give you! What do you mean, eating ice cream now, you trefniak! You've just had dinner!"

"Eh, can you call that meat? I've forgotten it long ago!"

Havah acts as though she had been stung by a fly. "What else?" she shouts. "The poor neglected children! It breaks one's heart to look at you! You're starving to death with me! You stuff yourself with three cutlets and—"

"Oh, stop arguing with me! You probably will keep it up till tomorrow! And meanwhile the ice cream man will go away—"

"A great dignitary he is, your ice cream man! A curse on him! Leading Jewish children astray! Where is the rebbe? It's just your luck that he isn't here, or he'd give you a sound spanking, so that all the tref ice would melt in you—"

"I-i-i-ice crea-eam! I-i-ce crea-eam!" the goy keeps on crying in the courtyard.

Abrashke squirms—what can he contrive next?

"The goy's ice cream is not made with milk!" he says. Then he tries to cajole the cook. "Havah, I'll help you mix the dough for the bread, you won't have to beg me! I will bring you the pickles, the sauerkraut from the cellar—"

"Thank you a lot! Why do you hang on to me like a tick? Where shall I get the money?"

Abrashke feels that Havah's voice has softened. "What?" he says, "You haven't five kopeks left from marketing? Why are you so sparing with mother's money?"

"So you think mother's money is trash? That it's to be wasted on the goy? And how will I give my accounting at night?"

"I-i-ce crea-eam! I-i-ce crea-eam!" The vendor's voice comes into the kitchen through the window.

Havah is bewildered, as though she were besieged from all sides. "Ai, what a brat! How can I get rid of him? He takes all one's strength! Here, rascal!" She grumbles while she rummages under her dress to draw out the purse. "Eating suet," she snorts. "Ordinary suet!"

HUNTING FOR CHOMETZ

Passover night is approaching, nearer and nearer.
Our apartment is all stir and bustle. The very air
throbs.

"Have you scrubbed here? And over there, in that
corner? See to it that the shelves are wiped clean.
Here are Passover towels!" Havah goads everyone
she can lay her hands on. "And you, Sasha," she cries
to the gentile maid, "go to all the black years with
your chometz! Take it to the cellar, you can eat it
there with Ivan!"

Havah gathers the last of the chometz dishes, crams
them all into a dark closet. These are things she uses
all year round, and now she does not even want to
look at them, she almost kicks them away. Suddenly
she stops, shuddering: a bit of flour gleams from the
black tin pan in which she usually bakes cakes and
rolls. "Where is your father?" she says. "If he were to
come, he'd burn even this bit of flour."

And she stores the pan away in the closet, so that
it should no longer offend her eyes. She scratches her
hands in trying to remove bits of red radish that re-

fuse to get out of the scraper. "What a nuisance, this chometz! There's no way of getting rid of it. Children, didn't the rebbe tell you to turn out your pockets? What are you waiting for? Soon your father will come to burn the chometz."

Havah proceeds to turn out our pockets herself.

"Oi, don't tickle me!" one of us protests. "You'll tear off my pockets with your hunting for bread crumbs!"

It is not easy to clean out one's pockets in one moment. All year round they are stuffed with everything that can be found in our house and in the street. So now my brothers are watching—they wonder whose pockets will have the most scraps sticking in the corners.

"Hush, father is coming!"

And the pockets are quickly turned in again.

Father has come to hunt for chometz. Havah's heart sinks. Father's face is serious, as though something had been lost in the house and he would have to look for it.

His black hat casts a shadow on him. Someone hands him a lighted candle. The little flame shines on his pale face.

"Have you got a feather broom?" he says in a low voice.

All the children follow him in silence. Everyone's breath is audible. Father, with the candle and the feather broom in one hand, and a wooden spoon in the other, brushes all the window ledges, the corners, the shelves, although they have just been scrubbed. He rummages in the bookcase, searches among the gemaras, searches as though someone were trying to conceal something from him. Suddenly he comes upon a crumb of chometz that despite the cleaning has remained hidden in a corner, or that Havah has put there by design, so that father should not have to make too long a search. His eyes flash—the flame of the candle blazes up too—as though he had found a treasure.

Next morning father gathers up all the crumbs he has found, places them in a paper bag, and carries them to the stove. The fire leaps on the bag. Father's eyes light up with the fire that devours the scraps of chometz.

"Thank God," Havah says, sighing, "we'll have a kosher Passover!"

PASSOVER EVE

THE first to be drawn into the Passover turmoil is Havah, our fat cook.

Since the day after Purim she has been going about in a daze. The ordinary weekdays have died away for her. She has only one thought in her head—to have a kosher Passover.

Distraught, in the early morning, she comes running to the dining room. "Children, you've dawdled enough!" she cries. "Finish your breakfast in a hurry, and get out of here! The painters have come!"

"The painters, already? Do you know when it will be Passover? Before Passover, even the Messiah may come!" my brothers grumble.

"And the place has got to be painted for the Messiah!" the cook says, aping them. "Instead of chattering, help me to move the cabinets."

"The cabinets! Only that? Just a little thing! It's incredible what she can think up, that Havah! Who can budge those cabinets?"

All together we heave against the clothespress. It budges. Inside it, black long coats are mingled with father's fur coat and mother's fox cape. The long hairs of the fur sting and tickle the other garments. We push the cabinet, it creaks and groans with each shove; its feet scrape the floor and leave a white mark behind them.

"Oi, enough, stop!" one of my brothers cries out. "You see, Havah, what you've done? One foot has bent. How shall we be able to put the cabinet back now?"

"O me, Lord of the Universe! What do you want of me? After all, the wall has got to be papered!"

"Perhaps you want to go to the rebbe and consult him as to whether we should not push away the whole wall?" my brothers taunt her.

"I've been as much of a wiseacre as you for a long time! Don't worry—I've got more brains in my heel than all of you together in your heads!" says Havah, getting angry. "Go to the rebbe, of all things! The question I should really ask him is how such heathen brats happen to be born into a Jewish family!"

"There she goes—Havah is angry already! Let's go!" The brothers pull each other by the sleeve. "Come on, let's go to see how they're baking matzah in town."

Suddenly Havah turns to the open door and calls out: "Reb Yidl, Reb Nahman, come in! You'll begin with the little room next to the dining room."

As though out of a mist two white shadows emerge; apparently they have just been waiting for Havah's

call. Two painters in white from top to toe. Everything about them—their shoes, hair, cheeks, and eyebrows—is spattered with white flecks as if with snowflakes. One has a ladder slung over his back, and in his
hand he holds a bucket full of paint. The other can
hardly manage with both his hands to hold a pack of
long rolls of wallpaper that look like bound-up scrolls.

The painters, as soon as they have come through
the doorway, tramp through the rooms. We push
away tables and chairs, clear a path for them—a company of soldiers might be marching in with them.
Soon they are in possession of the whole apartment.
One climbs up the ladder and scrapes the cornices,
the other clambers up on the table and scrubs the
ceiling with a coarse brush. Bits of plaster fall on his
head.

"Little girl, want to taste some lime?" the younger
painter asks, smiling down at me from his ladder.

His short little beard, stippled with lime, seems
pasted to his white lips. The painters make a jolly
time of it. Now one, now the other, bursts out laughing. They sing, whistle, stir the buckets, dip in the
brushes; paint drips and spatters.

Suddenly one of them begins to coat the ceiling,
back and forth. The other joins him, and both peck
at the ceiling with their brushes as birds would with
their beaks.

The painters attack the walls as though trying to
tear them down. The old wallpaper drops with a

rustle, dragging dried pieces of plaster after it. The peeled walls stand naked, scratched up and ugly. There is paint around my feet. The torn paper is scattered on the floor, and the painted flowers on it get wet.

The painters jump over the debris. They cut and paste new lengths of wallpaper with new little flowers. The paper crumples up, blisters, refuses to stick to the wall. Then the painters give it a slap with a wet cloth, and the swollen paper spreads up to the ceiling.

The little room, freshly painted and papered, shines as though decorated to welcome a bridal couple. But for Havah it is still not kosher enough. She covers the walls with white sheets, as if she were hanging talesim on them. Even on the floor she spreads a sheet. Now, it seems to me, one could bring the holy ark in there.

The first thing to be brought in are baskets of matzah—two tall, broad baskets, wrapped in sheets. It seems to me that each matzah is wrapped in a sheet. Havah, all in a dither, runs ahead, showing the way. "Slowly—stop here," she warns. "Here are a few stairs. Lower the baskets gently, slowly, so that the matzah will not break—God forbid."

She runs around the baskets, touches them, whispers as though saying a blessing: "Well, with the matzah a bit of Passover has already come into the house."

A third man, with a long, handsome beard, brings in a small basket of matzah shemurah for father. He

holds the basket in both arms, in the manner in which he would carry a Torah.

The man does not say a word. He notices a ceiling hook for a chandelier, and hangs the basket on it, so that no one should be able to breathe with a chometz breath on the special matzah. The basket is so completely swathed in white wrappings that the woven straw cannot be seen from any side.

From now on no one is allowed to enter the little room. Only Havah, in her felt slippers, may fuss around in there. She becomes the ruler of the little room and all the members of the family submit without a word.

When Havah goes through the apartment in a white apron and with a white kerchief on her head, it is known that she is going to the little room. Her face is tense, as though she were going about some world-shaking business.

We sneak up to the door, but she locks herself in. The latch clicks shut before our noses. We sit down on the little flight of steps leading to the room and hear a pounding of the wooden pestle.

"Havah!" we beg her through the keyhole. "Let us in! We'll help you pound matzah!"

The pestle pounds and pounds as if she were pounding on our heads. "Havah, we swear to you, our hands are clean. We have just washed!"

The pestle pounds more rapidly. Perhaps she does

not hear us. So we bang on the door latch at every thump of the pestle.

"Havah, why don't you let us also pound a little with the pestle?"

Suddenly the door flies open. We tumble back, almost rolling down the steps. In the doorway, like a storm cloud, looms the angry cook. She is unrecognizable. She is covered with flour; she could actually just have come out of a mill.

"Why do you bother me, all of you? Let me alone, you brats! What do you want—to pollute even my Passover, you good-for-nothings?" She is panting and her breath seems white with flour. "Of all things—to let you in to pound matzah with chometz hands! Are you too sick to wait till the holiday? Out of here!" She bellows at us and flour blows out of her nostrils. "Don't you dare to come near the baskets!"

She has vented her anger and returns to the little room. The latch snaps to with a bang. Again we press up to the door, put our ears to the keyhole. Now we hear something like the splash of a gentle waterfall dragging a mountain of sand after it.

"Havah, let us sift the matzah flour a little. Havah!"

The door flies open and she sticks out her head. "Will you stop or not? Will you let go of the door?" she yells.

A big sieve full of scraps of unground matzah rocks against her stomach. The flour drops from the sieve in a thin rain. It is as though the flour were coming out of Havah. One of my brothers turns over the sieve.

"Oi, you rascal!" Havah flares up. "May your hands dry up! You Tatar soul!"

She raises her hand, but stops, recalling that she is holding a Passover sieve with it. "Oi, my wretched years!" She begins to sob. "Lord of the Universe, even without this I don't know how to get on with all my work! Why are you pestering me? Who has asked you to come here?"

"But we want to help you."

"Never mind what you want! What sort of help would you be? And what makes you all of a sudden so attached to me? Bosom friends! Let's see which of us will get his way. Let anyone try to come near to this room, and I'll—"

An odd woman! Cursing all the time. When Havah gets excited it is better not to try to stop her. She might give one a couple of blows of such sort that— and she might tell the rebbe, too. She knows that both the rebbe and father will side with her—Passover must be kosher. So we let her alone.

She cools off and trudges back to the kitchen. At every step she leaves behind a white print of flour, like the tracks of an animal on snow. Soon we hear her coming back. Bending under the load, she carries on her back a keg full of beets. The keg sways, the beet liquor splashes, red drops trickle down on her path.

Havah toils hard. Her thick feet are swollen. Who

can help her? In her eyes everyone is tref. No one is allowed to touch anything.

"Havah, let us at least taste some beet liquor! It will be easier for you to carry it." We run after her.

She shakes her head. Her face turns from red to black. Her eyes are like sacks full of wet ashes. One squeeze, and ready tears will drop out of them. "Oi!" She cannot restrain herself; she sighs involuntarily. "Oi, my feet, they're killing me!"

Before she reaches the little room, Havah suddenly drops the keg. She stands there in a daze, making signs with her hands to show us that we must not come near the keg.

"Go, say you're sorry!"

"No, you go first, you'll do it better." My brothers urge each other.

Havah wrings her hands. "Who knows what state your hands are in," she wails. "Probably full of chometz!"

"Who? What? It's a long time since we have had anything to eat!"

And the keg is snatched from the floor. Havah sobs. If she could, she would make us kosher on the spot. "My God," she splutters, "those children! All they think of is to be feeding, to gobble up food!"

Then the little Passover room is filled with delightful goodies; it excites us and allures us.

Why should Havah alone taste all the good things

there? We begrudge her this. But Havah, like a cat, is on the alert—are we not trying to get in there? She fears to leave the little room alone. Perhaps she even sleeps there at night!

When we children gather in a little circle and whisper among ourselves, Havah at once looms up near us. "What are you doing here?" she asks. "What are you up to?"

"Nothing, we're just standing."

"Why are you standing in one place? You're surely going to go somewhere?"

"Not anywhere! Where should we be going?"

She mutters something, grumbling, and goes to see what is happening in the little room. Every day something is carried in there, now Passover sugar, now salt, or nuts, or prunes, or almonds. Linen sacks stand in all its corners. Havah seems to take pleasure in gathering together all these good things just to spite us and tease us.

A strange woman! On the very first day of Passover she always stuffs us so much that we hold our bellies. But now she torments our souls. And every day it is the same story.

Abrashke hangs around the door, goes up to it, runs away again. "Bashke," he reports, "I think they've brought raisins today!"

"No, I can smell prunes!"

Havah catches us red-handed. "What are you sniffing here for?" she asks.

"Can't we even sniff?"

"No, go wipe your noses, somewhere in a corner. What good is it to leave you here? You'll surely spare me the trouble of cooking something for the holiday!"

Now she starts on the task of purifying the pots and pans. Every day one or another of the copper pots vanishes from the kitchen.

All year long, all the copper pans and skillets stand arrayed on the upper shelf like generals on parade; they shine and glisten and cast fiery glances downward. Before Passover they have become tarnished, and Havah takes them down from the shelves by their black, smoked-up handles and drags them into a corner. Even the old Sabbath jug and the worn-out samovar into which not even a drop of water is put any longer—she has these made kosher in the same way as the samovar that seethes and boils days on end. Perhaps a speck of chometz will spatter out of them?

The vessels are made kosher by being lined inside with a new skin. Havah carries them to the little room, wraps each of them separately in a sheet. All these sheets seem to blow a little trembling breeze through the rest of the apartment.

"Bashinke, you're a big girl now, here is the key, go look over the dish closet," mother says.

"I think that last year a few wineglasses were

broken." Havah now orders us around outside the little room.

A special Passover closet is built into a wall in the dining room. Throughout the year the closet is locked. And one forgets that it is actually a closet. I open its doors. There is a whiff of an old odor. The locked-up plates, goblets, glasses awaken.

"What is missing, a wineglass, a cup?"

I climb up on a chair, stick my head into all the three compartments. I count the cups—will there be enough of them for everyone? I figure it out, as though we were already sitting at table, each in his place.

The dish closet sparkles. On all sides it holds glass and china, smooth, etched with gold. There is a shelf with cups. I am dazzled by all the glasses. Thick ones, thin ones, tall ones, small ones—they look at one another, reflecting each other like mirrors.

At one side there are red and blue Bohemian goblets; they stand as though in deep thought, in a world of their own. The smell of last year's wine has not yet evaporated from them.

Taller by a head than all of them, there stands, like an emperor, the cup of Elijah the Prophet. I touch it hesitantly. Every Passover I tremble lest it should burst with all the wine that is poured into it. Even when it is empty it sparkles with red lights like drops of wine. I fancy that I am sitting on a tree on which red and blue exotic birds are singing, and pecking with their beaks. The broad red bottles add more flame. Inside their red glass even plain water will turn red as blood.

What will happen when all the bottles and cups are put on the seder table, full of wine? The white table-cloth will light up. It will glow like a conflagration.

My weary eyes pass to another shelf. There stands a broad soup tureen with red flowers painted on it. The tureen is heavy; it is impossible to lift it. Now I understand why Havah's hands break under the load when she brings to mother the tureen full of soup with plump dumplings bobbing in it like children's bellies.

Next to the tureen are the plates, a whole shopful of plates! I pick out the small ones that are used as guest plates. To offer the refreshments is my task. I must plan on which plates I shall put preserves, on which the cookies, and on which the almonds. In the center of each plate there is a painted apple or pear. They strike my eyes, smell like real fruit. They con-fuse my calculations.

Suddenly I notice that at one side there stands, as if embarrassed, a milk pitcher with a broken-off handle. I look around—there is no other pitcher. If I go to the shop and tell mother that we must buy a new pitcher, she will reprimand me: "Why are you making my head spin with your pitcher? Here we toil like horses to earn a penny, and you in the house keep stealing and breaking things!"

Perhaps it is better not to tell mother. Where shall I get a blue pitcher like that to go with the blue sugar bowl?

When I go into the china shop I get lost there.

The shop tinkles with all the glassware on its shelves. I look at myself in all the glasses. In one I see half of my face; here my nose is stretched out, there it is flattened. Beside me is the owner, a tall, stout man. Through his black coat one cannot see the glassware. He moves lightly among his glasses, touches them with his eyes. From time to time he clicks his finger against a little glass. Does he do this to make sure that his merchandise is whole, or just to admire it, to show it off to me?

The little glass he touches gives off a tinkling note, like a voice on the air. The tinkle runs through the whole shop, and the vessels begin to vibrate. The proprietor removes his finger. The tinkle hides somewhere in a corner and is silenced. Only the steps of both of us can be heard.

I forget what I have come to buy. Havah has asked me to bring her something for the kitchen.

"Look," the shopkeeper whispers in my ear. "See the new liqueur glasses? They've just arrived. Pretty, aren't they?" He throws this in incidentally, and my head spins even more than before.

The delicate little glasses beckon to me, like tender flowers. One puff of wind could make them slide down from the shelf. They tease me with their sharp edges. I want to put them to my cheeks, my mouth.

Havah's voice is humming in my ears: "Liqueur glasses again? What for, for whom? There isn't even room to store them away. But for me you've forgotten to buy a couple of plain dishes. Why do we need such a liqueur glass?" And Havah raises it to the light. "Look, it will melt in water! How many such glasses have just crushed in my hands between the coarse towels?"

"But they're so pretty! I did not have the heart to leave them in the shop."

Let them scold me! These won't be the only superfluous things in our house!

THE SEDER

From early morning on I study the mah-nishtanah. Since I am the youngest child, it is I who must ask father the four questions.

"Ai! Every year you make the same mistakes!" one of my brothers scolds me.

"And why are there the same questions every year?"

It is an ordeal for him to teach me to recite the four questions. In my head not four but forty questions are thronging—but who would try to ask questions of father! I am chided all year round: "You clumsy fool, why do you keep asking questions all the time!"

But father is not here, so I can ask him: "Father, why do you become an emperor all of a sudden for the seder? Why is it that as soon as the first day of the half-holidays comes, you're no longer king, and our whole kingdom is gone? Father, why doesn't Elijah the Prophet sit beside you during the seder? He surely could be an emperor, for his cup is the

largest, the most beautiful. Father, why does his cup remain untouched in the middle of the table? Why doesn't he come at least for the recital of the plagues? Why doesn't he eat with us, and why do we open the door to call him only after supper? Father, why does he promise us each year, 'Next year in Jerusalem,' while he himself hides in the dark of night? Why, why?"

"Why are you turning in circles, you sleepyhead?" my brother berates me. "Here is your line, repeat it after me."

Once again, from the beginning of the page to the end, I repeat the four questions aloud.

Our apartment is in a turmoil. And I walk around slowly, as though I were carrying a pitcher full of questions on my head. I whisper them in a low voice. I am afraid that they may splash out from my memory.

The day goes by. There are odors of Passover foods, coming in, going out. Havah flies like a wind from the kitchen to the dining room and back. Every minute she stops. She keeps counting on her fingers.

"Charoset—" and she bends one finger. "Stuffed necks—" and she bends another finger. "The eggs are boiled. What else? Where is Sasha?" she cries out suddenly. "Just when she is needed, she isn't here. Seder or no seder—it's all the same to her. Bashinke, go and get her. She has probably gone to the cellar with Ivan. Their supper is ready." And Havah spits to one side, as though it made her sick to her stomach just to think of their chometz.

I run out and do not recognize our cellar. Its black walls shine. Sasha has emptied it so completely that it has become big and spacious. There is no rubbish. It no longer smells of kerosene, or of the mold of sauerkraut and pickles. The barrels are stored behind the wood. In the middle of the cellar a bit of a dining room has been cleared for the week of Passover. Here Sasha sits on a block of wood; she sits like a baleboste, and beside her, on another block, sits Ivan the janitor. A little tin lamp shines above their heads. It stands out a little from the wall; the wall is wet, but the chimney is so highly polished that the flame is fresh and cheerful. It bends sidewise, flickers on Sasha's white dress trailing on the bare ground. Her table is full of food. She stuffs her cheeks and does not stop laughing. Ivan, black-bearded—his sheepskin makes him look like a bear—keeps wiping his wet mustache.

"Ah, Bashutke, do you want a bite of chometz?" And he laughs coarsely.

"Sasha!" And I turn my back to him. "Havah is calling you! Everyone has come, and the seder will begin soon!"

I pull her by the sleeve; she ought not to be in the cellar alone with the drunken Ivan. She picks up her skirts, takes them in her hand, splashes a last laugh in Ivan's face, and runs out of the cellar along with me.

"Is it really true, Bashutke, that everyone is there? Hi-hi-hi! Come quicker!" The stairs bend under Sasha's feet.

Upstairs in the dining room the holiday is in full swing. The table stretches from one wall to the other —a white seder table in the silent light of red cups. A gleaming tablecloth stabs one's eyes. Candelabras shine. Tall white candles, still unlighted, quiver in the air. Even the ceiling shines, reflecting the polished chains of the chandelier. Each mound of matzah shemurah is wrapped in a napkin that looks like a four-tasseled talis-koton. Big white-covered pillows stick up in the chairs with embarrassment, puff at the matzah. The solemn bindings of the haggadahs gleam with their golden letters.

First mother comes in wearing her holiday dress. Her face shines. With her hair fluffed up she looks taller. Her dress is wide, long, trimmed with lace, buttons, ribbons; it trails on the floor, swishes, fills the whole room with its rustle. She goes to the candles, lights them, encircles them broadly with her two hands, as though blessing the whole table together with the candles.

It is now warm and light, as though not only mother's seven candles were lighted, but hundreds of candles all at once. Their warm fire caresses the cold gleam of the tablecloth, even as they themselves have just been caressed by mother's warm hands.

In the homes of the neighbors in our courtyard the

candles have also been lighted. The lights of all the people's candles cross one another. They seem to splash glowing gold. They are reflected in the windows, illumine the table; they play on the embroidered flowers of the tablecloth, on the bottles of wine that stand waiting. They redden the red cups.

Flame after flame licks the white table. It is not yet quite ready. It is being set. No one questions whether the table can bear up under all the things that are on it.

"Havah, have you peeled the eggs? Where is the salted water?" Mother bustles around the table; she wants to survey its whole length with her eyes, to see whether anything is lacking. "Hand me another pillow. I've quite forgotten that there will be another guest. Put on a new pillow case."

A couple of new pillows are spread. The chairs, like pregnant women, tilt their bellies upward.

"Mother, who is coming? How many of us will there be for the seder?"

"Ah," she says, waving her hand, "who would count them? After all, it's a holiday!" And then— "Quiet, they're coming from shul."

The murmur of an unfamiliar voice is heard. A guest comes in. "Gut yom-tov! How are you?" he says to mother. "Are these your boys? Are they bar-mitzvah?"

And each has his cheeks pinched.

The first comer is a distant relative of father's, a

peddler in neighboring little towns. He knows that to my father a relative is a sacred guest. So he has invited himself to our seder and behaves as though he were in his own home. He hums a tune, walks around, blows his nose loudly, moralizes, gives advice. To every new guest who comes he is the first to offer a broad welcome.

Now there is a noisy crowd, all waiting for father. To while away the time they tell each other stories, exchange jokes. "What are you studying now, Bashinke? Do you know Russian well?" someone asks me.

"Have you good marks?" my brother and my sister who have come from afar suddenly question me.

I look at them as though they too were strangers. I do not see them the whole year round. The brother is studying abroad. The sister lives in another city. This year she has brought her two little children. They crawl over everyone's knees, and especially if someone has long legs they beg him to give them "a ride."

All are merry. Only one old bachelor's eyes are sad, pensive. He looks at the boys at play. He recalls that he too once had a father and mother, a home of his own. And he moves over into a corner, like a little boy.

"Gut yom-tov!" Three little soldiers, all dressed

up for Passover, enter and stand in a row. The hubbub in the room has lured them in.

"Quiet, father is coming!"

The turmoil ends abruptly.

I do not recognize father at once. A new father!
In the doorway stands a white king, wrapped in white
from top to toe. He is lost in his broad white silken
cloak. The white silk shimmers, swells in folds. They
are held up by the thick belt. The sleeves hang down
like wings, long and wide, covering the hands and
the fingers. A white silken skullcap glistens on his
white hair. The whiteness makes him look broader
and stouter. There is a special radiance in his face.
A white fragrance comes from him. If father should
wave his arm, his sleeves would lift him like wings.
I look into his face. After all, he is an emperor today.

"Gut yom-tov!" father says.

"Gut yom-tov!" we all answer.

The seder begins.

Father occupies the head of the table by himself.
Against his two fluffed-up pillows he really sits like
an emperor on a throne. Following after him, the
whole company pushes to the table. They jostle one
another, shove the chairs, crowd to the table. Others,
on their big pillows, sit as though raised on high.
Father is the first to remove the napkin from his seder
setting, and casts a sharp glance over the things arranged before him. Mother's eyes stop—has anything

been forgotten? Under his yellow matzah shemurah, sticking out, like bits of moss from an old roof, are branches of spice, a little mound of maror, a roasted stuffed neck, a hardboiled egg. The other seder settings, arranged like father's, are uncovered too.

"Arke! You'll give me all of your bitter herbs, won't you?" Abrashke suddenly cries across the table to his elder brother.

"Ah, you lubber, you're interested in only one thing! Holiday or no holiday, all that's on your mind is food!"

"And you—why are you barking like a dog on a holiday? After all, it's bitter herbs I'm asking for!"

"You're ready to stuff yourself even with bitter horseradish! Do you think I don't know you! Ha-ha!"

"Quiet!" father chides them. "What kind of uproar is this? Pour wine into the cups! Serve them to the guests!"

Bottles of wine pass from hand to hand. The guests snatch them in turn from each other. The wine bubbles, splashes on the tablecloth.

"It's good wine, indeed!" Someone has had time to swallow a drop. "May I have luck as good as the wine is sweet!"

"Ah, ah!" says another. "Elijah the Prophet's cup!"

Father nods. Mother throws in: "Take wine from this bottle! It is a better one!"

A bottle is tipped; Elijah the Prophet's tall red cup,

which a minute ago was standing silent, pensive, is filled to the brim.

The wine begins to foam. I am dizzy from the strong wine smell that comes from the cups. Suddenly it is as though a wind were blowing from the opened haggadahs, stirred up by the fluttering of pages. All heads are bent over the books. The first benedictions are pronounced.

I sit in my accustomed place, squeezed in between father and mother. Because of father's pillow, my corner is more cramped than usual. I feel hot and choked. My head is heavy from the wine. The pillows lure me, I want to put my head on their soft down. But I know that soon, after a few phrases, father will bend over toward me, as though the four questions were being addressed not by me to him, but by him to me. Now he is beckoning to me: "Come, the questions!"

Suddenly there is silence. Everyone looks at me. I hide my face in the haggadah. My head whirls together with the letters. I move my finger on the page, I want to straighten out the lines. I swallow my breath, I am startled by my own voice: "Wherefore—"

Father prompts me in a low voice. It seems to me that at the other end of the table they are choking with laughter. I get snarled up even more. I crawl from one line to the next, I mix up my questions. Yet I have memorized them so well, and I had so many things to ask! I have no sooner spoken the last word than a shout rises. Relieved, they have all turned to the haggadah.

The company is like something that has started off on wheels. Each recites for himself, tries to go faster than another. One tries to catch up with the other, to drown his neighbor's voice, to push him with his own voice.

The voices echo back from the windows, clamber up the walls, awaken the portrait of the old Rabbi Shneurson that has hung in our house for years. The rabbi looks down with his green eyes and listens to each voice as if he were testing everyone. On the other wall, the portrait of the aged Rabbi Mendele cannot remain quiet either. Pensive, wrapped in a white cloak, and with his long white beard, he comes down from the frame as though he had been called to the reading. The bare walls prick up their ears, the ceiling comes down, listening to the haggadah; it has to carry each word upward.

Page after page, the words pour out like sand in the desert. I am tired from looking at everyone. Where are we?

My brothers race ahead as if they were in harness.

"You lout, what are you reciting?" Suddenly a non-Hebrew word resounds. "You've skipped several pages!" This is Mendl chiding Abrashke.

Whom is he going to cheat? And why all the haste? Little mounds of letters and lines stand up, run up and

down as though on stairs. I lose my way in my haggadah. I touch its yellowed pages. At one place I find
a wine stain, at another a piece of last year's matzah.
Then suddenly I come to a page with a picture repre-
senting a seder table, with emaciated faces around it.

I feel an ache in my heart. Here they are, our
grandfathers, our dearest grandmothers. How weary,
how dried up they are! I stroke them and turn page
after page. I look for them everywhere. The piece of
matzah crumbles over my haggadah. It is as though
the sand of the land of Egypt were grating under my
feet. I murmur: "We were slaves—"

The crowded pages begin to choke me. In my ears
the wind of the desert blows. The pale shadows of the
colored pictures come closer to me, breathing into my
mouth. I no sooner touch them with a word than they
pour out their hearts, their sufferings, relate how they
trudged in exile in the desert, tarried, and trudged on
again. Days, nights, years, without water, without
bread. My soul is drawn into their cycle as though by
a spinning wheel. I hear their steps. They sweat,
tramp, with stooped backs.

My own shoulders are heavy; I too am dragging
myself over the deep sand. My mouth is parched. I
find it hard to pronounce the words. They paste my
lips shut—they feel like lumps of clay. I whisper, bend
over, try to get into the haggadah, join the long trek,
walk with all of them, say a word to them, help them
to carry something—

Suddenly it occurs to me to wonder with a start: Were there children with them? They must have cried, wailed.

Where are we? It seems to me that all have lost their way. I shall never catch up with them! What passage is father reading? I ought to listen to him. His voice is calm. Each word falls on the table like a measured step. He walks on a smooth road. I should like to walk in step with him. Thank God, he has stopped for a minute to catch his breath.

"Now, the plagues!" He makes a sign with his hand beckoning that something be given to him into which to pour the wine for enumerating the plagues.

"Water made blood. Frogs—"

Father sounds like a bell. Each plague is pushed away, a long drop of wine is poured over it. It is as though father wanted to push each trouble as far away as possible. He has poured out his whole cup.

Mother takes the little jug and slowly performs the same rite. She is embarrassed lest she name the plagues too loudly, she fears to spatter the table. Each holds his cup in his hand, as though ready to give battle. Each grasps the jug, pours wine into it from the cup; they seem to be spitting into the enemy's face. Everyone aims at the middle of the jug, trying to hurl his curse straight to the heart. The plagues fall like bullets to the bottom of the jug. The jug comes to me last. So many plagues are bubbling in it! They have become as thick as spittle.

[233]

"Water made blood. Frogs. Lice. Murrain. Here, here, take it"—it is as though I were hurling stones. I pour the wine, I splash it. I cannot stop my hand. The clay jug grows into a clay head of the evil Pharaoh. I would gladly pour out all the plagues on him at once, break my cup against him, cover him with the blood of red wine.

"Locusts. Darkness—that's for my grandfathers and grandmothers you persecuted. Firstborn slain—that's for the tortured babies"—I am terrified by the curses, by the red stains on the tablecloth, and hurry to pour out all my wine.

ELIJAH THE PROPHET

EXHAUSTED from eating, from the haggadah reading, we chew our morsels of hard afikoimen.

Only father conducts himself as befits an emperor.
Reclining on his pillows, he chews the afikoimen with
closed eyes, as though he were thinking: "Whither
will He lead us now?"

Suddenly he opens his eyes and casts a glance at
mother. She moves her chair from the table, opens her
haggadah, takes a half-burned candle from the candelabra, and turns to me: "Come, Bashinke, and take
your haggadah with you."

I jump up as if stung. My heart is oppressed—with
awe and with exultation, because only I accompany
mother to go to meet Elijah the Prophet and open the
door for him.

Each with an open haggadah in her hand—mother
holds the burning candle too—we go quietly out of the
dining room. The men remain sitting at the table. No
one budges. Each one looks at us, escorts us with his
eyes, as though they were all blessing us, their envoys.

We walk quickly through the dark parlor in order not to be late, God forbid. That would be the supreme mischance—that Elijah the Prophet should pass at our house and find the door closed. The little flame, which seems to sweat from our hurry, hardly lights the way for us. The candle drips tears—perhaps it is afraid of the surrounding darkness. We come to the little entrance hall. My heart pounds; it seems to leave my body, to soar up to the sky and drop from terror to the dark floor.

"Take care, cover the candle!" mother says to me hurriedly and pushes open the door to the street. The black night rushes in, like a wind, blows into my face and my skirts, almost extinguishing the candle, and shaking us.

"Now," I think, "Elijah the Prophet is quite close. He is probably coming right now. The air is fluttering with the motion of his flying carriage, he is waving his wings, his spirited horses are catching up with a cloud."

I am afraid to look out from the doorway, lest something should catch on my clothes. From underfoot shadows run forward. I see only a patch of sky. It gleams like black velvet. It makes the street black. In the black sky, a little star splashes like a fish in water and spatters light. Suddenly it looks in at the door. It has stopped right over our heads.

Mother's eyes are lowered. She does not see anything. And what if the little star should fly in at the

door, and Elijah or even the Messiah himself, with one leap, should appear behind us?

I am on edge, I listen. Everywhere there is silence. Silence hangs from the sky, hangs over the street, over the houses. Not a step is to be heard. The lanterns burn each with a thin little flame.

In the house across the way, through the windows, there wanders a reflection of a burning candle. Is there a door open now in every house? Is there in every doorway a mother with a little girl holding a candle in her hand?

Suddenly there is a noise behind our backs: chairs are being pushed from their places. Perhaps the whole table has fallen apart. It is the men. Hearing us open the door, they have all risen from their seats and are reading the haggadah in voices so loud that they seem to be trying to rouse the night itself.

We stand there feeling buried under their voices. I move very close to mother, I want to cling to her skirts, so that when the black night drags us away we shall at least be together.

The little candle, wide awake, bends, sways to all sides. I put a hand around it, screen it from the wind, so that it should not go out, so that we should not, God forbid, remain in darkness facing the open black hole of the doorway.

Mother quietly recites from the haggadah; perhaps, she feels, the silent night will listen more attentively to her quiet prayers. Her lips are barely moving, her face is wrinkled up, her spectacles slide down from her nose. The candle goes out. It seems to me that we are standing here forgotten.

I place my head under the haggadah, under mother's hands—with her ardent blessings falling on me, I shall not be afraid any longer.

"Elijah the Prophet," I pray, "have mercy on us! Come down quickly! It is cold, dark. Come to our house! Everyone is waiting for you. And you'll be warmer too. Do you hear how my father is praying? He never cries, and today he is praying so loudly. Come then, Elijah the Prophet, come!"

A streak of light passes across the doorway, cuts through the air. I want to raise my head, to see what mother is doing, what is going on in heaven. My eyes are suffused with darkness, there is no way of opening them. I feel that I cannot stand the light; it makes my eyes blink.

"Next year in Jerusalem!" A last cry comes from the dining room.

Again the chairs have been pushed up to the table, and there is silence.

"Mother, has Elijah already gone into our house?"

"Next year in Jerusalem!" She throws the words into the open doorway as though in answer.

I look out into the street. The wind has subsided. The sky is studded with stars, big ones, little ones, come from all the ends of the world. They hang like lighted candles with their heads down. Their rays of light crisscross, one enhances the other, and all of them together sway like a canopy under which soon the white moon will come like a bride in all her glory.

Having closed her haggadah, mother makes a sign with her hands, stroking the air—she might be bringing something down from heaven. Perhaps? Perhaps? She does not want to go away from the open door. She strokes the air for the last time—it is like a kiss—and closes the door.

We go back silently. The cool night blows on our backs, taking us by our shoulders with its hands of air.

In the dining room it is light and warm. All of them are sitting with lowered eyes, humming the haggadah passage. No one gives us even a glance. Mother silently sits down. The humming air envelops me, surrounds me with the old haggadah pages.

I turn my head back and forth—has Elijah the Prophet been here? The fluttering of my heart flickers out.

THE AFIKOIMEN

"SASHA," says mother to our gentile maid, "here, give this cup to Ivan."

"*Spasibo*—thanks!"

We hear from a distance the thick voice of our watchman, who is supposed to protect us from thieves and robbers.

"Will Ivan drink the whole cup of wine?" I think to myself with fear.

"Fill the cups," father calls out.

We resume reading the haggadah. A voice rises and dies out, as though falling into a well. One reader hums quietly through his nose, some others hurry; they probably want to eat.

Father rises from his seat first. He goes to wash his hands. The children mix up all the haggadahs. There is a jostling at the washstand; the jug, the wet towel are torn from one's hands. There is once more a rush to the table. They catch the pieces of matzah that father distributes for the blessing; the hard pieces jump over the table until they are stopped by the hands that snatch them up.

"Here, Bashke—you like maror?" And father gives me a second portion of it.

I spread it thickly between two pieces of matzah and chew the bitter tidbit. Egg yolks crumble under mother's fork and yellow the salted water. Everyone sips his spoonful of the mixture with wrinkled nose.

Meanwhile I forget to watch where father hides the afikoimen. His pillow is full of down like a stuffed belly—how can I look for it? Now the fish is being served. Mother's hand is stretched over the table. Everyone holds up his plate. Then the knedlach come; they are easily swallowed with the yellow soup.

"Who has a dumpling to spare? Give it to me, to me!" the children beg one another.

"Hurry up with the meal. Otherwise it will be late when it comes to the afikoimen," father urges us.

He is resting from eating. Sated and tired, we are longing to go to sleep. We look at father. For some reason he squirms in his chair. He turns over his pillows, looking for the afikoimen.

"Ah, you brats, you did manage to steal it!" And he smiles.

I sit like one cheated. I did not see either where he hid it or who stole it. Annoyed, I look at one, then at another.

"Aha, I have stolen it despite everything!" Abrashke cries out. He holds high the afikoimen. His eyes gleam.

"Fine, fine, now let's hear what you want for it!" father says.

"Oh, I won't give it up unless, unless—"

Here Abrashke in his eagerness begins to think up some very great gift. I look at him, frightened, almost glad that I have not stolen the afikoimen. For I would only have asked for some little thing. Such audacity— in the middle of the year no one would open his mouth to ask for even a trifle. But father, like a real emperor, does not even think of bargaining.

"Well, that's too bad! But you're not a fool. You'll get what you want. But now hurry up and give me the afikoimen. It's getting late."

Merrily we bite into our pieces of hard afikoimen.

TISHAH B'AV

I SPEND almost all summer in the village. Hosts of flies hum. Through the branches the sun comes in brilliant little circles. There is no way of catching them, the little moons. They jump out of one's hands, from under one's feet, they do not let themselves be trampled on. Here in the village I forget the city. It seems to me that I myself am a blade of grass, a plant.

I walk around barefooted. I begin to smell of earth, of rain water. I lie like a red berry at the edge of the field. Blue little flowers, like blue bonnets, lure me, wink at one another among the full ears of corn.

I go into the woods, I clamber over the tangled roots of the trees that have been felled. I look for blackberries and I gather them in a little basket. I look at my bare feet. They grow longer, thicker. I stuff myself with sun and air. I do not notice how days and nights run by, how the sun is running away somewhere, moving ever farther off and sinking deeper, and every evening casts a longer shadow on the earth.

"Bashke, come back, tomorrow is Tishah b'Av"—thus mother sends me word from the city.

I am glad. It's a long time that I have been away from home.

"Oh, how you have grown!" Sasha will cry out.

Mother, concealing her joy, will just glance at me—so that no evil eye should strike me, God forbid.

Gaily I come to our house and stop in the doorway. Has someone died? Why is everyone weeping? Why has mother told me to come home? I have fallen from a bright sky into a dark pit.

I stand and look at mother, who sits with lowered head, reading a supplication. She weeps silently, does not look at me. The long white tablecloth is stretched like a corpse on the empty table. In the candelabras the burned-out candles are melting. A couple of books lie between them. Father stands at one side. His white socks strike the eye. It makes my heart ache.

Dear God, why are they all so gray and black? It is summer outside. The sun is shining. Gentile grown-ups and children are running about, laughing. And here?

On low stools, as on stones, father and mother sit mourning. They are like stones, petrified. The floor is covered with sand and dust. Tears stream from their eyes.

What sins have my parents committed that they must pray to God in this way? What misfortune do they lament? My brother Mendl says to me sorrowfully: "We deserted our holy Temple. It was burned. Our land was ruined. It is the ninth of Av."

Sadness comes upon me. The little red and blue flowers are still blooming in my eyes. One blow has dispelled my warm summer.

Abrashke comes running in and pulls me by the sleeve.

"What are you standing here for?" he says. "Come to the courtyard, we'll throw pine cones at each other!"

I feel quite indifferent. I allow myself to be dragged to the yard. Abrashke has prepared a whole pile of cones. If all these cones hit me, I shall be scratched to bleeding. I hold my hands over my eyes. Abrashke is now firing the cones as from a gun. They get into my hair, stick to my dress. I find it hard to move.

"Abrashke, that's enough! Now let me throw a little too!" I am almost in tears. I grab a handful of cones. "Here, here! Now I'll hit you too!"

I tear the prickly cones from my dress and throw

them at Abrashke. I throw and throw. I do not see what my brother is doing. And he? He calmly gathers them together and pastes them on himself like buttons. He sticks a cone on his cap. His whole chest is studded with cones.

From the open windows there comes a choked lament: "How doth the city sit solitary! Shall never joy return to us?"

A WEDDING

BEFORE sunset it is always gloomy in our house. Everyone stays in the shop till late at night. All of them have drunk their tea long ago. The cold samovar stands as though its soul had flickered out. The chandelier hums. Long shadows stretch from it over the table. All day long the dining room has been full of hubbub. Now it is like a dark abyss; I am afraid of falling in.

I fancy that if I remain sitting like this, the chandelier out of anger will pull me up to itself. And if I cry out, who will hear me? Even the glasses still standing on the table will not budge. I am afraid of the lamp and the cold samovar. I am afraid to look at its brass belly. Across it my pale face is spinning.

If only someone would come! Where are my brothers? Where do they run about every evening? In the streets there is wind, frost. But they come home cheerful, with a booty of freshly gathered stories.

"Abrashke, where have you been?" I ask.

"Not anywhere," he throws back.

"And what have you done, Abrashke?"

"Nothing!" And he laughs.

I sit at the table, prop my head on my outspread hands, and look into my brothers' open mouths.

"Ha, ha, ha!" one brother interrupts the other.

"What piece of news are you telling me here, you horse's head?"

"But I saw it with my own eyes!"

"You stupid fool, you think that because you saw it, it was true? I know that man better than you do, I—"

It is gay when my brothers are about—I am never afraid. I envy them. They can go wherever they want to; mother won't scold them. But I? Where shall I take myself? To the kitchen? I am weary of the kitchen. All day long it is saturated with all kinds of food. And it must be dark there, with the little lamp. No, I won't go to the kitchen.

Shall I go to the shop? There it is certainly light and cheerful. But the moment I stick out my head from behind the curtain, they will yell at me: "What do you want? Go home! We've got plenty to do without you."

I am always a nuisance. This I must leave alone, there I must not creep in. So I drop the curtain and take myself away. I stumble into the entrance hall. I see my coat hanging on the half-dark wall. My white hood protrudes from its sleeve. Should I try perhaps to go out into the street?

Half-dressed, I run down the staircase that leads to the balcony. A tall, dark stairway looms up behind my back, like a black snake.

Quickly I push open the big door. A white, snowy path opens up before me like a sky. The cold tickles my nose. A thin snow scatters fresh, light little pearls. I fill myself with the fresh air as if it were water. It is quiet in the street—the snow has buried all the voices.

In the white, snow-covered lanterns frozen little flames are burning. The drivers stand at the curb like mounds of snow. Their horses seem not to be breathing under their wet sacking. They scarcely seem alive. Only a few people are walking in the street. The white snow creaks under their feet. I start walking too.

I run along the wide street. From a distance I see a big, lighted courtyard. In the middle of the courtyard there is a two-story house. Through its windows one sees long, spacious rooms—wedding halls.

Every night a wedding is celebrated here. Even from outside, the house looks like a lofty hall. Two large candelabras hang high in the air; like two lions they hold up the balcony. Today too there must be a wedding. Whose would it be?

The snow is falling around me, thicker and thicker. A ball of snow drops from a candelabra. It splashes like a tear at my feet.

I hear steps. Who is coming? I watch. People are approaching from a gate. They are dragging a large copper siphon tank that sprawls like an uncouth animal on the shoulders of a couple of men. They come closer. A little stream of soda water spatters into my face. I jump up. Should I laugh or cry?

"I don't bother you, what have you against me?" And I sneeze into their faces.

"Ha, ha, ha! A strange girl—she likes weddings and washes herself with soda water!" They whinny.

Waiters come, one after another. They carry various things, one a soft cake that still gives off its warmth, another a jar of pickles that gurgles in his hands; still another bears pans containing large sponge cakes.

Tables are dragged in. Wide boards sway in the air between pairs of legs.

"What are you carrying?" I want to see everything.

"Do we know? It is all kinds of foods—challas,

stuffed fish, whatever your heart desires, little girl," the merry waiters say, smacking their dry lips.

I move to one side to let them pass. Doors fly open before them. The tables, as they push them in, blow the cold air to all sides. Chairs stand scattered along the walls. One corner is fenced off with palms, like a little garden. Under their green shadows stands a tall chair, rising high like a throne. A red rug lies there. The tall chair is waiting. What bride will sit in it today?

I look at the chair. It is an old man with sunken cheeks. From its emaciated cushion sparse fringes hang down.

How many brides have sat on that cushion? Each bride has left in it her fear and her tremblings.

All the other chairs can be moved about, but the high throne with its sunken cushion stands in one spot, waiting. What is it waiting for? It is waiting as for a light in the darkness—for the white bride.

Not until the bride comes will the chair come to life. It will breathe, it will fill itself with air and whiteness. The carved heads on its back will bend toward the bride. And when the bride sighs, the chair will utter a groan. And when the bride melts into tears, the chair will embrace her with its uplifted arms, because the bride, whether she is pretty or ugly, will burst into tears in its arms and readily pour out her heart.

The chair is ready. As the bride raises her hand-

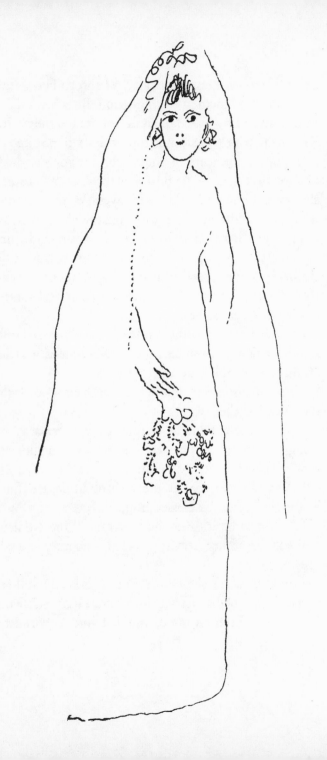

kerchief to her eyes, the chair will absorb her warm
tears and store them in the old wood. But only a delicate chink, a tiny little hole will be bored in the chair.
The bride who will sit in it tomorrow will not know
anything of the tears of today's bride. For she does
not see anything; she approaches the chair as though
she were blind, with lowered eyes. When she sits
down, her white veil is spread over the chair. And as
if she were lifted on two wings, she is suspended in
the air, ready to run away to another world. And so
the bride does not feel the tears of her sister of yesterday. She sheds her tears on the old chair and leaves
her bit of weeping heart.

But where is she, the bride? The tall chair still
stands empty. It is embarrassed. Everyone is a little
afraid of it. People take a detour around it.

Women jostle one another in the halls as though
they had lost their way.

"I wish the ceremony were already over. May it
bring good fortune. This day is somehow dragging as
though it were made of pitch."

"What do you say? A pretty little bride, eh? She
really deserves to be blessed by God!"

"Amen, so be it, may she be happy!" the women
whisper, breathing heavily in their smoothly ironed
dresses.

But why hasn't she come? She is probably still at
home. She is being dressed in white. Her black hair
has already been brushed, braided into a coronet.

Young, white hands, and older hands, furrowed with veins, fuss over her hair.

"Hand me a pin! Have you got a pin?" one woman asks another.

"Come, Manichke, you're well educated—you'll be better at pinning the veil on the hair," they call to someone.

What does she look like, the bride? Isn't a bride just a long white dress that drags over the ground like a living thing, with an airy veil floating after her? Through it, seen as through glass, the bride looks remote, far off.

Perhaps even now she is riding through the dark streets. Her veil falls from the narrow sleigh and merges with the blue snow. Her old mother is coming with her, holding her fast—she does not want to let her flesh and blood go from her arms. Was she not once also a bride, so white, so young? The sleigh glides on.

"Are you not cold, my child? Take care, don't catch cold!"

I too begin to feel cold. I see—something has blown past the windows, as though a silken dress had gone by. Have I missed the bride then?

I look around. Waiters spread broad white tablecloths, which fall with a rustle on the long tables. They spread in a flood, they cover the black floor beneath them. The waiters laugh, run, jostle one another. Plates, spoons, forks clatter on the tables.

"Let the stuffed fish pass!" a scrawny fellow sings out and wriggles like a fish; on his tray there glistens a shining tail.

"And my chopped liver!" another waiter shouts.

"Here is a dish of petcha, make way, make way!" The helpers push about.

Around me is the stir of guests arriving. The stairs groan under their feet. Every woman who comes in fills the air with her panting breath. I squeeze my way through them. I run down to the balcony. I would rather wait here for the bride. I want to see how she will jump down out of the air and put her feet on the ground. I hide in a corner. People's furs shake their collars full of snow down on me. White beards turn black. From wet woolen shawls there protrude women's fluffed wigs—little women studded with flowers and pearls. Single snowflakes like little diamonds remain gleaming in their hair.

The snow is melting under my feet. I feel wet and cold. A sleigh glides up to the balcony. Is this not the bride?

A couple of stuffed sacks roll out from it—little girls with red little faces.

"Oof!" They blow into their gloves.

Their tangled shawls unroll. Bare shoulders, naked arms appear, and dazzling pink and blue dresses. These must be the bride's sisters. They flutter in all directions. They squeal. "Rose," shrills one, "see how

pretty it is here! Oh, so much light! I don't see anything!"

"Rivke, quick, look up—what's going on up there?"

"That's right, children, go up to the hall. You
might catch cold here—God forbid!" The older
women push them away.

Indeed, the women need this room for themselves.
Their fox mantles fall from their shoulders like gates
opened wide. The furs twist about and smack me
with their warm tails.

No one pays any attention to me. They know there
is a little girl here wrapped in her hood; she stands
like a stranger and looks on. I feel embarrassed. I look
at my weekday dress. A pity that I did not change
into another dress! I look up to the lower stair; under
the raised skirts one can see long white stockings
reaching up to the buttocks. Let them have a good
time, the short little girls, let them jump with their
white legs! I cannot restrain my tears.

I am annoyed because I am not one of the invited
guests at the wedding. I would have been dressed in
my pink silk dress. Sasha would have brushed my
long pigtails and tied them with a flowered ribbon.
My dress would lift lightly as soon as I stood on the
tips of my black patent leather shoes. When the music
began, I would stand in the middle of the hall and
shove my feet as a little goat snuggles its feet into
grass.

If I had come with my brother Abrashke, we

would be asked to dance a *pas de quatre*. "Be so kind as to move aside a bit," they would say. "Let the children dance. It's such a pleasure to watch them!"

All the guests sit in a circle about the hall, making a ring with their outspread skirts. I bend one leg. My shoulder too is bent, as though I were falling. Then I glance at Abrashke, and at once rise on the tips of my toes and look in another direction. Abrashke holds me fast. Several times we bend and rise again. The little violin plays. Suddenly a drum begins to sound. The lamps blaze brighter. I do not see any faces. Only the women's bellies sway in rhythm. They smile while they do this, trying to help us as we dance. We seem to be carried away in the air. I throw back my disheveled hair, like a shadow that has crept into my eyes.

Then the music goes drunk and pounds out a mazurka. There is no way of holding back one's legs. Abrashke stamps his feet and tosses me in all directions. It seems to me that we have jumped over the hall, that we are dancing somewhere else. The mazurka stops as suddenly as it began. We remain standing.

Hands drag us toward them.

"How old are you, little girl? Ah, but this is Alta's youngest!" And they stroke our necks.

"May they be spared from the evil eye, good children as they are! That a boy should be able to dance so well!" And they pinch our cheeks.

[258]

The music has stopped, as though forever. I feel cold. The air is gradually cooling. A cold wind has begun to blow into my face. I am still standing at the open door. It has opened wide. Through it comes a mountain of snow. The mountain straightens up and scatters snow like rain. A tall man grows out of the white mountain.

"Well, it's Bashke! What are you doing here? Hasn't the bride come yet? Let's go upstairs. Why are you standing here in such cold? Ooh!" He blows on his frozen hands. "What, Bashinke, you don't recognize me? Wait, some day I'll lead you to the canopy too!" And he bursts into laughter.

Everything shakes about him. I look at his Adam's apple jumping up and down. Of course I know him—he is the jester. I stand waiting for the bride, and he has come for the wedding.

He takes me upstairs. He inhales the wedding air through his long nose. His ears dance. He shakes his head. His head is all tuned like a violin, ready to be played. Then why does everyone burst into tears when he, who is merry, calls out, "Let us bless the bride!"

He gets into your soul with his voice. He knows everyone's family. He knows every aunt, every cousin. He knows whether the bride has a father, a mother. He knows what is happening in everyone's life, what is going on in anyone's heart. As though he had a rope in his hand, he pulls each person into the middle of the hall and plays on him as on chords. One by one he calls out the names of those who must bless the bride. The name echoes for a long time—until the aunt who has been called heavily crosses the big room. Is she still on her way? She totters a little, as if she were full to the brim of benedictions.

When the jester raises his voice, everyone's heart is crushed. His voice trembles even more, and everyone is frightened, as though the aunt were approaching a corpse.

The lighted candles held around the bride are quivering. The bride sits like a frightened white bird. The aunt comes closer, raises her arms as when she blesses the Sabbath candles. The bride lowers her head even more. Blindly she gropes for her handkerchief. Now her soul will surge up and pour itself forth in bitter tears.

Her aunt pities her. She does not touch her. She blesses her from a distance, like a star. The jester looks at everyone, quickly calls out other names. People catch their breath, blow their noses.

All the guests comfort the bride. They cool her with fans. They straighten out her veil, which has twisted awry on her head. They blow at the hair that sticks to her forehead because she is perspiring.

Squeezing my hand, the jester drags me up the stairs.

"What are you doing? What are you doing?" he

quacks, as soon as he appears in the doorway of the hall.

The circles of women disperse. I slink along the wall.

What is that? I rush to the door. A white cloud rises from the stairs. A light wind begins to blow. A little violin cuts the white air and curls it into a sweet melody. The cymbals and the drum have slipped in, panting.

Now she has come, the white bride, light as air. With every step she takes, her heart lifts. The musicians play above, below, at the side. They cushion her path. On the last step she stops. Should she go farther?

People have crowded back to the walls. Even if she were blind she could walk to her throne. She looks at her white slippers gliding like boats over the floor.

I stand glued to other people's backs. We push one another as though we wanted to roll the bride up to the high shore.

At some distance a row of men is drawn up. They are dressed in black. At the head of them a young man walks with trembling steps. His high hat too trembles on his head. He comes closer to the bride's whiteness. The bride, it seems, is afraid of him, and he of the bride.

In our hands we hold gaily colored confetti. The jester sings. The men accompanying the bridegroom come closer and closer. The red rug is now entirely covered with black shoes. The bride draws herself up

[261]

and waits. We keep behind her. The bridegroom with one twist of his hands throws her white veil over her; he might be throwing it over himself—as if he were lifted in the air with his bride.

We scatter our confetti on him, like stars from heaven. We scatter it on ourselves.

Like a cloud covering the black floor, the bride remains alone. We rush to her. We no longer see her face. She is supported at her arms, at her sides.

A little red sky has spread in the middle of the hall. It is supported on big poles. The bride, almost fainting, is led to the canopy.

GLOSSARY

Afikoimen (*H*, afikoman)   the piece of matzah eaten at the conclusion of the seder. The afikoman is hidden by the father, later to be "stolen" by the children

Balebos (*H*, baal ha-bayit)   the head of the family; a householder

Baleboste (*Y*)   the mother of the house; a hostess

Barinke (*Y*)   lady

Bar-mizvah (*H*)   a boy who on reaching his thirteenth year becomes a "son of the commandment," i.e., reaches religious maturity

Challa (*H*, challah)   the white bread eaten at Sabbath and holiday meals

Charoset (*H*)   the mixture of ground nuts, fruits, and spices, symbolizing mortar, eaten at the seder

Cheder (*H*)   elementary Jewish school

Chometz (*H*, chametz)   leavened bread, proscribed at Passover

Chumash (*H*)   the Five Books of Moses (Pentateuch)

Etrog (*H*)   a citrus fruit used in the synagogue at Sukkot; pl. etrogim

Gabbai (*H*)   a collector; a director of the synagogue

Gemara (*Aramaic*)   a part of the Talmud

H indicates that the word or phrase is derived from the Hebrew, *Y* that it is from Yiddish.

Goy (*H*) nation; gentile

Goyish (*Y*) gentile (adj.)

Gute Woch (*Y*) "A good week": greeting at the conclusion of the Sabbath

Gut yom-tov (*Y*) "A good holiday": holiday greeting

Haggadah (*H*) the book containing the story of the exodus from Egypt, read at the seder

Hakkafot (*H*) the carrying of the Torah in procession on Simchat Torah

Hanukkah (*H*, Chanukkah) the Feast of Lights, commemorating the rededication of the Temple by the Maccabees

Havdalah (*H*) the benediction at the conclusion of the Sabbath and holidays

Kapporeh, pl. kappores (*H*, kapparot) "atonement": on the eve of the Day of Atonement each member of the household swings a fowl over his head while reciting penitential prayers. After this the fowl is slaughtered and the value of it given to the poor

Kiddush (*H*, sanctification) the benediction at the commencement of the Sabbath and holidays

Kittel (*Y*) a ceremonial garment

Kosher (*H*, kasher) fit for consumption according to the dietary laws; proper; in accordance with Jewish ritual

Le-chayim (*H*) "For life": a toast with wine or spirits

Machzor (*H*) a holiday prayer book

Mah-nishtanah (*H*) "What is the difference": the phrase introducing the four questions asked by the youngest child at the seder

Maror (*H*) the bitter herbs eaten at the seder

Matzah (*H*) the unleavened bread eaten during Passover

Matzah shemurah (*H*) unleavened bread prepared with especially strict observance of the Passover regulations

Megillah (*H*) scroll, in particular the scroll of Esther

Melammed (*H*) a teacher, especially in an elementary Jewish school

Mezuzah (*H*)   the scroll inscribed with biblical texts that is attached to the doorpost in the Jewish home

Mikvah (*H*)   ritual bath

Mi-sheberach (*H*)   "He who has blessed": introductory words of a benediction

Musaf (*H*)   the additional prayer recited on the Sabbath, New Moon, and holidays

Pesach (*H*)   the Passover

Purim (*H*)   "casting of lots": the holiday commemorating Haman's fall

Raboisai (*H*, rabbotai)   gentlemen

Reb (*Y*)   a colloquial title of address

Rebbe (*H*, rabbi)   rabbi, teacher

Rebbetzin (*Y*)   a rabbi's wife

Rosh ha-Shanah (*H*)   the New Year

Seder (*H*)   "order": the ceremony carried out in the home on the first two nights of Passover

Selichot (*H*)   prayers for forgiveness on the days preceding Rosh ha-Shanah and between Rosh ha-Shanah and Yom Kippur

Shabbes (*H*, Shabbat)   Sabbath

Shalesh sudes (*H*, shalosh seudot)   the three meals of the Sabbath; usually the third meal eaten on the Sabbath afternoon

Shames (*H*, shammash)   the caretaker of a synagogue

Shehecheyanu (*H*)   "He who has sustained us": a benediction on special occasions

Shemoneh Esreh (*H*)   the Eighteen Benedictions in the three daily services

Shikse (*Y*)   a gentile maid

Shkutsim (*Y*)   rascals

Shochet (*H*)   a slaughterer according to the Jewish law

Shofar (*H*)   the ram's horn sounded on Rosh ha-Shanah

Shul (*Y*)   a synagogue

Siddur (*H*)   the order of prayers; a prayer book

Simchat Torah (*H*)   the Feast of the Rejoicing of the Law

Sukkah (*H*)   a hut inhabited on the Sukkot days, to commemorate the wandering in the desert

Sukkot (*H*)   the Feast of Tabernacles

Talis (*H*, tallit)   a prayer shawl; pl. talesim

Talis-koton (*H*)   a small tallit worn as an undergarment

Tashlich (*H*)   a ceremony carried out on Rosh ha-Shanah, symbolizing the casting off of sins

Tefillin (*H*)   phylacteries, i.e., scrolls inscribed with biblical texts that are worn on the arm and head during the daily morning worship

Tishah b'av (*H*)   Ninth Day of Av: a fast commemorating the destruction of the Temple

Torah (*H*)   Book of the Law; the Bible, especially the Pentateuch

Tref (*H*, terefah)   forbidden food

Trefniak (*Y*)   one who eats forbidden food

Yehudim (*H*)   Jews

Yom Kippur (*H*)   the Day of Atonement